AMERICA OVER EASY!

T0164394

MARK SHEEHAN

Photographs by Shane Boocock, Bridget Willis
and Holly O'Sullivan

NEW HOLLAND

Preface

It occurred to me as I was assembling my thoughts on a working title for this book, that America is a smorgasbord for the visitor, and if you see the landscape, topography, time zones, accents, and all the other ingredients that make up the great American menu, you'll realize there's an awful lot to it.

Even ordering your eggs in the USA has a ritual wrapped around it. If you ask anyone who has ever visited America, you'll hear them wax lyrical about ordering a simple breakfast there. For the initiated, breakfast eggs in America come in at least a dozen different varieties, each with a colorful description. My preference has always been eggs-over-easy. But there are strong corridors of local support for scrambled, sunny-side-up, eggs in the window, poached, eggs in a blanket, hard-boiled, fried, baked, and even the occasional egg-beaters, to mention only a few of the eggy American options available.

Once eggs are ordered, you still need to settle the issues of bread, buns, or muffins, your preferred coffee, skim, 2 per cent, or full cream milk, style of potatoes, and the degree of cooking for the bacon, ham, or sausage. This is followed by the selection of fresh juice options. Ordering breakfast in America is fun and easy once you have the insiders' information in hand to help.

Like ordering breakfast, visiting America IS easy, as long as you know the way forward. We've written this book so you can make the most of your time while there, and make the most of the 'menu specials' this unrivaled destination has on offer. Bon Appétit!

Read on. Dig deep, take notes, ask questions, let your fingers do the walking on the Internet and ask anyone who's ever been to the USA for their views and suggestions. By doing this, you'll soon discover your very special journey to the United States of America began, and was enjoyed, long before you ever locked the front door, hoisted your luggage, and turned off the lights.

Most guidebooks tell you what to see and do, and help you to get around when you've arrived. Our view is that to make the most of any holiday, the fun begins with doing the homework—the excitement of planning, getting the best value for your hard-earned holiday money, and locking those 'must-do's' down firmly. A trip to the great USA can be savored long before you arrive in America.

With this book in hand, we hope you'll take full advantage of the taking on of the USA, and enjoying your own version of America Over Easy! The tone is intended to be 'conversational' and we welcome your questions and feedback. The website references have been placed in the body copy on purpose. If you pick up and set this book down, you can simply go online straight away, instead of attempting to sift through and cull the relevant contacts from the index listing at the back of the book. And please, drop us a line—we'd be more than happy to help: www.overeasyguides.com.

One final thing before you get started: If anyone ever tries to tell you they've got the full or definitive story on travel to the USA, they're lying! America is not only massive, it's constantly in a state of change, which makes it a truly 'moveable feast'. I get some of my best information and updates from people who've gone to the USA after me, and have taken the time to update the information.

America is so huge, that anything you say about it is true...
...And the opposite is probably equally true
James T. Ferrell

Acknowledgements

There was a child went forth every day.
And the first object he look'd upon, that object he became,
And that object became part of him for the day
or a certain part of the day,
Or for many years or stretching cycles of years.
Walt Whitman, 'Leaves of Grass'

I've been traveling professionally for most of my adult life, and it's only in the past 20-odd years of it that I've begun to truly experience the places I've been fortunate enough to see. I give full credit for this eye opening to my parenting partner Bridget, and, in my more recent travels, to our three magnificent offspring: Cody William, Dylan Thomas, and Hayley Catherine. Our children have inherited their mom's keen interest in taking the path less-traveled, peeking around the corner, tapping the 'local guys' on the shoulder, and in the most pleasing of ways, prying open my senses to places we visit in the process.

I can't thank my troops enough for the opportunity to tag alongside them (I'm usually driving but they're all exceptional navigators) as they scratch below the surface, engage locals, and in general soak up the best of anywhere they happen to invade.

I've also got to say this book never would have been possible without the introductions and information culled from the travel writers' bible, TravMedia. TravMedia is the brainchild of Australian, Nick Wayland, who cleverly assembled a Fort Knox of information specifically for the travel media. The website offered me contacts and high resolution images that enabled me to simply move the mouse about and connect instantly with 'American authorities' and travel experts when doing my research.

Another whopping big thank you goes out to all of the visitors and convention bureaus that provided information, and in some cases, the colorful materials and images for the book. Each venue wanted us to pass along a hearty invitation, and to ask you to not simply take my word for it, but to go and savor the USA for yourselves.

Someone seriously smarter than me coined the expression 'You only get out of it what you put into it' and I've begun applying that notion to my travels. Prior to turning over this new leaf, I was a paid travel scribe, a hired pen. I went from pillar to post in North America laying down the tape, marking off the mileage, concocting the cute trivia bits, and writing hundreds of paint-by-number, crib-sheet guides for the hundreds of other tour directors and trek leaders who followed in my tire tracks.

I was very good at my work, scratching below the surface for travel trivia, digging up the funny facts and the juicy bits that the tour director could pass along from the front of the motor coach, but I'd never really drilled into a place. Nor had I stopped to talk to the people I encountered in droves until I had the good fortune of running into Bridget Willis.

Bridget took me to places I'd been a dozen times before for the very first time, and at a far more human pace and perspective. She removed my ever-present wristwatch along with my unspoken schedule of ETA (I used to try to better my 'estimated time of arrival' when revisiting venues). In doing this, I remained completely oblivious to the 'road less traveled', which Bridget opened my eyes to. I'm extremely grateful to her for this, and for raising three magnificent kids who seem to share her explorer's enthusiasm as part of their genetic make-up.

CONTENTS

Author's Notes

If the USA is a menu, it is a virtual smorgasbord with offerings that will appeal to every traveler's palate. Although the USA is a massive menu, one of the nice things about it as a vacation destination is that you'll never have to travel very far between bites. From appetizers to downright gourmet offerings, the United States of America has got it all.

The handsome Masai of Africa have a saying, which is a series of tongue clucks and almost yodel-like vocalizations, which suggests: 'To eat an elephant, take one small bite at a time.' Fitting advice for anyone headed to the USA.

Years ago, a chocolate company in the USA called Whitman's had a problem in that they had so many varieties of chocolates that consumers were stymied when it came to making a selection. So they created a mixed box, called the 'Whitman Sampler', which had a variety of chocolate yummies, with a small description of each on the top of the box. In this way, chocolate lovers worldwide could take small bites of everything on offer, without having to buy a single flavour in bulk.

Our suggestion for digesting the best of America is to sample America in small, well-paced bites. Linger longer locally. Like a good meal, you need to savor it properly. Visit the USA at a reasonable pace, focusing on an area or region instead of trying to do it all in one go. America must be consumed in reasonable bites, or you'll race around skimming the surface and be hungry in the end for more. Plan in advance. Take small steps and then you'll have ample time to truly uncover the real America. If it takes you three or four more trips to the USA to take it all in, so what? It's a whopping big place, and there is way too much to see and do in one visit. Even for those visitors who have time on their hands, it's more than a mouthful or a month full. A massive billboard sign at the entry to the town of Hondo, Texas proclaims 'This is God's country, please don't drive through it like hell!' Slow down and you'll have more time to digest the great U.S. of A.

Most visitors to the USA from the Pacific Rim arrive on the West Coast. Alternately, arrivals into the USA from the UK, South Africa and Europe first touchdown in venues like New York, Boston, Orlando and Miami along the US Eastern Seaboard.

America is a massive piece of real estate. The 'lower 48 states' (the ones that are all connected to each other) are about the size of Australia, and that's if you leave off the two dangling bits, which comprise the handsome Hawaiian Islands and the Enormous State of Alaska.

I think someone's actually sat down and figured out that you could also, with room left over, drop the UK and New Zealand

Take your time ... there's a lot on offer

So much to see! Start planning early

into the USA some 34 times, and even the self-proclaimed 'World in One Country!' of South Africa fits into the American footprint about 39 times without a shoe wedge. We're talking BIG!

Americans are very proud of their landscapes and historical areas, and with the help of federal and state funding more than 17 million acres of national park lands have been set aside and protected for citizens and visitors alike to explore, ponder, and experience. America boasts over 6,850 National, Historical, provincial, and regional parks—all of which are open to visitation and some of them are bigger than entire states or countries.

Setting aside big chunks of the country for everyone to enjoy is a relatively new notion. In fact the USA led the way in 1872 when Yellowstone National Park became the world's first national park. Cutting into parts of Wyoming, Montana,

'Take only photos and leave only footprints.'

No matter where you are, chat up the locals

and Idaho www.rockymtnintl.com, Yellowstone is home to a large variety of wildlife including grizzly bears, wolves, bison, and elk. Preserved within Yellowstone National Park are Old Faithful and a collection of the world's most extraordinary geysers and hot springs. The formation of Yellowstone for public access and enjoyment eventually led to more than 100 nations following suit and establishing their own national parks and reserves.

No matter where you are, chat up the locals. Over the years I've been invited to join a parade float, attend a barbeque with the Governor of South Carolina, compete in Cow-Chip Tossing competitions (sun-dried cow turds for the uneducated), co-host a local TV program, crack a Budweiser with Ted Turner (Jane Fonda's ex and CNN founder), take the helm of the Staten Island Ferry, take a spin on the back of Jay Lenos' NBC back-lot Harley and much more... by simply putting my hand up and making myself available. So go on, don't be afraid to use your accent and break the ice.

Introduction—Setting the stage

Thirteen stripes for the 13 original colonies, 50 stars for 50 American states

Use this guide and consult with your travel agent in advance of any American trip. The book is intended to point you in the right direction for information, without spoon-feeding you all the little bits. Your trip will be like none other, depending on what you make of it and we know you'll get a whole lot more out of the Americans and America if you take ownership of the planning process.

Travel trivia can oftentimes be a fast track to a nap for readers, but I like the comparisons, if taken in small doses. So if my take on the statistics bores you, simply move onto another page.

> *There's lies, there's damned lies*
> *and then there's statistics!*
> Samuel Clements (aka Mark Twain)

Overseas guests just love visiting the United States. Why wouldn't they; there's a lot to like about a place that boasts over 9 million square miles to tramp about n. Some statistics just floor me, especially when it comes to overseas visitation.

In 2012, more than 1.1 million Australians visited America, compared to only 550,000 Yanks who visit the 'lucky country' of Australia. Australia's population idles around 23 million while at last count, the Americans boasted a population of over 300 million. One of the reasons for this disparity, we think, is in the distance between the two continents and the time it takes to get to and from them. On average Americans only get 2 weeks off each year for 'vacations' and getting to and from Australia might drill into those precious days in comings and goings.

So not only do 1.1 million cash-carrying consumers from Australia visit the great USA each year, but also when they do visit, Australians linger longer than any other nationalities on the planet, staying a whopping 22.9 days on average, and they spend more money than any other group while in the USA. Shopping is the number one activity for long-haul visitors to the USA—a fact that keeps Americans smiling and cash registers ringing. Australians also boast the highest 'return rate' of any long-haul international visitors. The 'average Australian' will visit the United States 3.2 times (I'm not sure how you get a .2 rating!) in a lifetime. In short, they come in significant numbers, stay longer, and return to the USA with gusto.

Australia is number 6 on the top ten list of international visitor numbers, more than remarkable given that Canada and Mexico share common borders with the USA where in many cases, visitors can simply 'walk across'. Warm relations between the USA and Australia, New Zealand, South Africa, and the UK, and a common language (with pleasant modifications on both sides) all help to set the stage for a visit to the America.

New Zealanders, although far fewer in population numbers, are just as excited about visiting the USA. With a total population of only 4.7 million, the kiwis consistently land over 135,000 strong on American shores. They too, linger considerably longer than other international visitors, get into many more of the nooks and crannies of the United States and spend up while on American soil. Proactive New Zealand airlines, travel agents, tour operators, and wholesalers offer a wide variety of products and services that have special appeal to New Zealanders. Simply march into any retail travel agent and you'll soon discover a significant portion of the wall and display cases are lined with things-to-do-American.

The welcome mat is out everywhere in America

Enjoy the view of America from every angle. You're on vacation.

For South Africans, the lure of 'the land of the free, and the home of the brave' is addictive, even if the costs are somewhat higher. With a population of over 47 million people, a whopping 90,000 South Africans visit America annually.

With most arrivals firmly anchored on the eastern seaboard city of New York, it will come as no surprise that Southern African guests linger a fair bit along the east coast of the USA for the first taste of the States. Cities such as Boston, New York, Philadelphia, Miami, Washington DC, and Orlando take top honors. Other keynote attractions that lure the 'lakka' Southerners include the call of mother nature to venues such as The Catskills, The Shenandoah Mountains, Vermont's ski areas, the Florida Keys, New Orleans Jazz, Elvis Country, and Everglades National Park to name drop only a few.

For visitors from the United Kingdom with a population of over 60 million people, over 4.5 million of them invade the USA each

Steeped in history

year, and the number is steadily growing. Fueled by plentiful and frequent airline seats and cruise options, America is easier than easy for the British holiday-maker to access. Top the UK's relative proximity to the States with very seductive airfares and you've got all the ingredients for great getaways. Gateways such as Miami, Orlando, New York, Boston, and Washington DC welcome the European community and UK with open arms, especially as they ring cash registers totaling in the billions of tourism dollars. With over 4 million visitors each and every year pouring into America from the UK, attractions, car hire companies, accommodations, and others have lined up an attractive shopping mall of opportunities that cater to this audience. One of the major calling cards for UK travelers to the United States is its sunshine and warm weather.

Come on in ... the weather and the water's just fine!

Hands-on Help

1. What to take and what to leave behind

In business, we talk about 'The Five Ps' which, when you drill into it, is simple: 'Proper Planning Prevents Poor Performance'. This makes good sense when planning a 'tops-trip' to America. Try www.ustraveldocs.com.

The basics

Before I go to the US, there are a few things I have to put in order before I close the front door and turn out the lights. For example: a valid passport and, if necessary, a visa. This area of entering the USA has gone though some significant changes in the past few years, and we've set aside a place in future chapters to drill into how it all works.

Here are a few suggestions on what to take along, and what should be left behind. Packing for a trip is a bit of an evolutionary process and should not be undertaken with 10 minutes to spare while the taxi is waiting at the curb. I open up my suitcase a good two weeks before departure, finding an out-of-the-way place where I can simply toss items into the bag for possible consideration. Then, periodically, I review the pile up and discard items I know I won't need, or can get my hands on once I'm in America.

I focus on what activities I'll be undertaking and this helps me shortlist a lot of items I need to get me underway in the USA. For example, if my trip is taking me to the frozen tundra of Alaska, or the ski slopes of Aspen, I'm going to want a starter's set of cold-weather gear. Likewise, if your trip of a lifetime to the USA involves white-water rafting and a stint in Las Vegas or Death Valley, I'd be packing shorts, T-shirts, swimmers, and other desert and warm-weather gear.

For my toilet kit or basics, I love buying them 'over there' so I only pack for a few days on the ground until I can pop into a local supermarket or drugstore for more. I fill up my bags with those cute hotel soaps and shampoos I've pinched from previous trips to see me through until I hit the shops. Trust me, you'll be stymied by the magnitude of personal hygiene options available on the shelves in America.

Most importantly, plan to pack light. You will need the extra space in your suitcase (many visitors buy another one in the USA) for items you buy and bring home. Nowadays, restrictions on what you can carry on board change regularly, so it's a good idea to keep it simple. If you do require medications, be sure to have alongside proper prescriptions and medical notes if questioned. Immovable restrictions on liquids and containers have recently been implemented so it is imperative to check with your airline of choice beforehand to avoid having to forfeit items at security checkpoints. No sharp objects, illegal drugs or contraband items (the USA still has an embargo on Cuban cigars) will be allowed aboard with your in-flight items but again, know before you go what you can take in checked bags versus carry-on requirements. The American Transport Security Administration is the most up-to-date source for information, try: www.tsa.gov.

I take along a top-pocket traveler's 'punch-list' every time I go overseas. I'm not good at multi-tasking so whenever I travel, I create a list of 'must see and do things' that make up the cornerstones of each American trip. I simply pack with this list in mind, ticking off items I'll need along the way. Everything else simply falls into place. The list serves two important purposes. It highlights what I'm going to do as a broad-brush plan and it leads the way for what essentials I need to pack.

Practice and pack your accent!

Practice your best rendition of 'G'day Mate', your 'Jolly Good', your 'Lakka-likea-Crackka!' and your 'Sexteen' in front of the mirror.

Your accent will deliver you instant celebrity status in America. Locals will roll out the red carpet, and you'll be rubbing elbows and other body parts with the locals before you know it. At the very least, you'll get asked a few questions about your home country, and reminded to 'have a good day!' with gusto.

A major faux pas made by well-intentioned international visitors to the USA is to ask your newfound American friends if they know where your home country actually is! Most American school curriculums insist on geography and history instruction, with a very provincial emphasis on things American. So unless you want to embarrass your new buddies, don't ask. For many Americans, you just might as well say you're from another planet,

Use your accent—the locals will love ya!

All of America is an 'Amusement Park'

but they'll have you reading the newspaper aloud because they 'just love that accent'. Our general rule of thumb is to use your accent to break the ice, and get the locals chatting. Then jump straight into asking questions about sports, local weather, or the venue for the best of something—that is all it usually takes. Your accent and out-of-town status can actually be a whopping big bonus.

Being an American, I take great pride in being able to make my way around the States and knowing all the rules, especially in places like LA where I've had some significant mileage under my belt. On a recent trip to California with my family, and in keeping with my mood, I saw a break in the roadway divider and did a U-turn right in front of a California State Trooper. With lights flashing, he pulled me over. A shaky start to our American holiday. I rapidly produced an ear-to-ear grin, and with my best 'g'day matie' and Vegemite-oriented Australian 'accent' handed over my Australian driver's license. The State Trooper casually leaned into the window and said, 'Krikiee Man! Who do you think you are, the Crocodile Hunter?' Needless to say we avoided a citation (ticket). Moral of the story: Use your accent on the locals, obey the well-posted street signs, and teach the children to say little or nothing when Dad is talking total rubbish to a copper.

Even as an American I sometimes think I need a translator; particularly when I'm traveling in the Deep South, New York, or the coastal New England states. I once introduced one of my very proper British friends to a local in New Orleans. We were in Pat O'Brian's bar (a must for their original 'Hurricane' cocktails) on Bourbon Street in the French Quarter when our new found Louisiana friend said with an ear-to-ear smile: 'I bees from NOLINs, I stays on my momma and I loves pull'in' on my Dixie! Wanna crack one with me?' To which the young, lovely, and impressionable British gal turned to me and whispered: 'Please, call me a 'bobby' . . . I think I've just been verbally molested!' In translation our new acquaintance was saying in his very best Sunday southern drawl that, he was a native of New Orleans, he lived at home with his mother and his favorite pastime was drinking his beloved DIXIE beer. His offer to 'crack one' was an offer to buy the lass a bottle of beer. Americans speak the same language, English; you just might not recognize it straight off.

For an overseas visitor's view on the Americanisms and regional accents go to: www.richard-seaman.com/USA/Life/index.html for this New Zealander's informative take on Yank speak. We'll be waiting at www.overeasyguides.com to hear your insights on the American accents.

2. Getting there and back—Air, land, and sea

Most arrivals in the USA are accomplished via major international airports and gateway cities. Be sure to shop around for airline tickets and packages that provide a value-added angle and deep-pocket savings. A huge savings tip to take note of is to buy in bulk. There is not a single airline that will offer you a 'mate's rate' or deep-pocket discount for the airfare component alone—it'd be airline hari-kari to do so. But you can save hundreds, sometimes thousands of dollars by purchasing your air-and-land content as a 'package' whereby hotels, airlines, transfer companies, and attractions can camouflage the deep-cuts and discounting when buried in among the other components of the package. For example, you can pre-purchase your car hire, 3 nights in a hotel on arrival, airport transfers, a CityPass™ www.citypass.com, plus entry to an amusement park along with your airfare sometimes for $100 less than the stand-alone economy airfare. Buy packages before you go and save. We've had friends 'in the know' that will oftentimes purchase a value-added package deal and toss away some of the unwanted inclusions because they've already saved heaps. Another great advantage to booking these dynamic packages is that you'll know before you got that you have a big part of your spending and budget covered off already.

Buying as much land content (anything other than airfares) as you can beforehand reduces the on-the-ground surprises or unexpected additional damages inflicted on your credit card or ATM card while enjoying the USA. Keep in mind when shopping about that many airfares and packages have terms and conditions that might have restrictions once booked and paid for. Also, some promotional air passes and airfares can't be purchased once you're in America.

The options for getting around are endless

３. Visa, entry, and document requirements

Every visitor to the USA will need a passport, which is valid for at least 6 months' longer than your intended visit, and a return airline ticket. New legislation called the 'open skies act' and the 'visa waiver program', have made it easier to enter the USA for visits of under 90 days, but carry restrictions. You'll want to check this out www.ustraveldoc.com, especially if you've had a recent run-in with the law or a felony conviction.

Another area that could send up a red flag for entry to the USA might be triggered if you have 'overstayed' your visa on a previous trip to the USA. One thing is for sure, entry to any overseas country is a lot more defined after 9/11, and upgrades are regularly in the works with optical identification, fingerprinting, and other additions to the customs and immigration process. If you have any queries or doubts about your status for entering the USA, it's best to sort yourself out beforehand, and then simply have your passport and other documents in order on arrival. It might just take you a few minutes longer than in previous years. Besides, other countries have already, or are about to implement, the same measures.

Not all countries are part of the visa waiver program, so it is best to check with the US Embassy in your home country in advance of an intended trip. Start with www.travel.state.gov or a visit with your local travel guru to get the most up-to-date facts on what you'll need. Other great sites to peek at are www.thebrandusa.cp, and www.seeamerica.org from which you can extract specific information for your home country. The other way to get this information is via the USA- based website of the same group on: www.discoveramerica.com. The Tourism Industry of America Association boasts over 7,000 active membership companies and is also another great source of

English spoken here, even if you sometimes need a translator

information. Try: www.tia.org. Another significant change in travel to the USA is the establishment of part-time work for non-US citizens in America. Organizations such as CCUSA (Camp Councilors USA) have been set up to provide work experience in America, while other organizations can now apply for and be granted seasonal work permits for agricultural jobs, ski areas, and winter-time employment. Age and education requirements are necessary, and some of these firms collect a small fee for doing the paperwork and acting as in-country contacts for participants. Go to www.ccusa/com or search 'working in the USA' for other options.

If you intend to study and attend classes in the USA during your visit, you need to check on any special visa requirements with the US Consul-General in your home country. The best place to start is online at www.unitedstatesvisas.gov.

Bring money—you'll want to spend up big in the USA

You may, although it is highly unlikely, have to prove you have sufficient funds to carry you while you are visiting America. Credit cards, ATM cards, travelers' checks and cash can be presented as proof. It is also a good idea to carry along a printed itinerary of your agenda or paid-for land arrangements.

DO NOT attempt to enter the USA with a visitor's visa and gain employment! If caught, you'll be deported without ceremony. Penalties are high, and you'll have near-impossible odds of ever being allowed back in. And DON'T overstay your visa: if it says 90 days, it means 90 days. I recently met a well-heeled and retired Australian who was traveling around America in a rented El Monte recreational vehicle. He was staying in the USA for 89 days, and then popping over the border to Mexico and Canada for a peek while his vehicle was being serviced, only to return to the USA after a week away and continue his road trip.

4. Time zones and seasons
What time zone today?

America is so vast that it has required a series of 6 distinct time zones to satisfy the need for sunshine hours. Along the 'lower 48 states', there are Pacific, Mountain, Central, and Eastern time zones with Alaska and Hawaii having different times zones from the mainland states. In 1918 America also adopted a 'daylight savings' to its clocks, so at 2am on the second Sunday in March (spring forward) and reverts to standard time on the first Sunday in November (fall backwards) adding or deleting an hour. Be sure you check with the locals so as not to be caught out by an hour with flight connections or event kick-offs. To confuse matters further, on numerous Native American Indian reservations, tribal members may well have their own more organic take on the local time. You might be in the State of Arizona where the local time is high noon, yet at the tribal Navajo nation trading post, it's

Go ahead! Jump in feet-first

one or even two hours earlier. In most cases, you're not likely to be in any hurry to blast through, so stop looking at your watch. Check out www.worldtimezone.com/time-us.

To every time, there is a season . . .
Biblical Song Lyric (Byrds)

North American seasons

The USA enjoys four seasons: spring, summer, fall (autumn) and winter, each having its own special allure.

Spring is generally known to be the months of April and May: frost-melt, new plantings, farmers busy in the fields, and the inevitable 'spring cleaning'—garage sales and 'white elephant' offerings. Groundhogs and bears come out of hibernation. Track-and-field sportsmen, tennis players, and golfers line up for an early shot. For my money, this is a great time to travel because it's often referred to as low or 'shoulder' season and rates are seductive, lines shorter, and you can save some serious dollars. The staff will have more time to stand around and chat you up in Spring, as they anticipate the onslaught of summer crowds. 'April showers bring May flowers' is a long-standing rhyme of the season.

Summer is generally known as those months of June, July, and August: warm to hot weather, afternoon thunderstorms. Colleges, universities, public and private schools are out for the summer. Traditionally this is the period when Americans themselves take to the open road for a 'vacation'. A good bit of harvesting is done during summer and a new activity, tornado chasing, has become popular in the Midwestern States. Beach and water-related activities, baseball and softball games, and outdoor sports rule this season. Points of interest and attractions have their highest visitor usage during the summer, so high

Any time is a good time to visit America

season rates will apply in most venues. Lines might be a tad longer and, in general, there will be more families and young ones around.

Autumn is generally September, October, and November with New England fall foliage and colorful leaves high on the visitation list. The Americans are back to the grindstone and school, and in many places it is 'sweater weather'. Gridiron football (shoulder-pads, helmets), lacrosse, and soccer are favored during this season. With the exception of places where they boast a bountiful 'fall foliage' and changing of the leaves, this period is great value offering shoulder or low season rates. Fall is a great time to travel in the USA because school holidays are ended, Americans are back on the job, and you can have the run of the place for less. The weather tends to be mild, and the water is still plenty warm enough for swimming.

Winter months are traditionally attributed to December, January, February, and March. There'll be snow skiing and winter sports, cold weather and cold-weather clothing in layers.

America is massive: enjoyed no matter what the season

Basketball and hockey rule the nation during this season. Try 10-pin bowling, offering up lots of locals to meet in the bowling alley. Ski resorts are getting top dollar for beds, and major cities are charging holiday shoppers like wounded bison in the lead up to Christmas and New Year. There are still plenty of good deals to be had in winter. In the Northern USA, pack for cold weather, or be ready to buy some new clothing. Shop up!

5. Money, credit cards, and tipping —Pack the plastics

I've got just one word for you kid, Plastic!
From the movie The Graduate

Yes please, bring plenty of 'plastic': The Americans live on it. Visa and MasterCard credit cards are accepted almost everywhere. American Express cards are widely honored, but because of what retailers refer to as 'stiff fees' charged to merchants for the privilege of swiping an AmEX card, they are not as well liked as the others. I also contact my credit card providers before an extended trip to the USA, letting them know that I'll be charging hard on the card overseas soon because some credit card fraud-monitoring departments will put a temporary 'stop' on a card that appears to have significant usage in a previously unknown overseas venue.

Oh yes, lest I forget, if you leave home with only your Diners Club or Discover Card in hand, you'll starve! The Diners Club card, once well exposed throughout the USA, is almost non-existent when compared to the options for using the other big three. Carry one of each if you like and you're more than amply covered, especially when you hit the shopping opportunities head-on and the run on your card limit gets hot.

Your ATM card is also a great way to use your money and bank-friendly ATMs appear everywhere. However, don't put all your faith in this means of getting to your money. Always have a pocketful of small denomination US dollars within reach, especially on arrival in the USA.

Money matters! The American greenback

The basic unit of currency in the United States is the dollar ($1) or 100 cents or pennies, and still referred to by many as a 'greenback' for obvious reasons when you look at one. Coins are minted in 1 cent, 5 cent (also known as 'nickels') 10 cents, (aka 'one thin dime') and 25 cent pieces known as 'quarters'.

Also floating about are two coins which seem to not have endeared themselves to cash registers so they are not in high circulation: the 50-cent piece, and the 'Susan B. Anthony' $1 coin. Although still accepted as legal tender, they are not widely used or circulated so as a visitor to the USA, smile nicely at your American bank teller, and ask if you might please have one of them to take home as a souvenir. They will be collectable one day.

Paper money in America comes in a number of different denominations, but it's always the same size, and up until fairly recently, the same color! In recent years, the Americans have made color concessions and additions to their currency to prevent counterfeiting so new bills are being introduced with variations on the 'greenback' theme. They are, however, all the same size. The key difference in each bill is the American statesman pictured on the green side (the other side is black) and the value for each one. If your vision is impaired, or you've had a big night out on the town, we suggest you scrutinize your bills before handing them over to the cabbie or to pay the night's

Go ahead—bite the bullet and buy It! You may not be back for a while

tab. It's not uncommon for first-time visitors to hand over a $100 note, thinking it was only a 'tenner.' If you want the lowdown on the dosh beforehand, try www.banknotes.com. American paper money (bills) are produced in $1, $2 (very rare now) $5, $10, $20, $50, and $100 denominations.

Americans think your currency is a lot like monopoly money

Please don't bring your home currency to the USA—Americans don't know what to do with it. If they do offer to make an exchange, you'll pay hefty exchange rates and commissions.

Best bet? We live in a different world, where not that many years ago visitors would stock up on travelers' checks in a variety of denominations to cash as they went. However, with the arrival of ATMs almost everywhere, you can extract your own cash at the curbside as and when you need it. Check with your bank beforehand to be sure they allow for international withdrawals for your ATM card, and ask about fees for withdrawing your own funds while overseas. Some banks charge a small fee for ATM transactions and it is well worth it. Before leaving home, contact your bank for their international   contact details in case you have any hiccups.

A few words of warning about ATMs

I once escorted a film crew from Outrider Films in the UK that was filming a feature on motor coach tours. On the very first day of departure, Gordon Swire filmed the tour director as he spoke to the group, and advised everyone we would be leaving the hotel for Las Vegas in 30 minutes. One hapless Australian went to the hotel's ATM, put in his new card, and incorrectly entered his password. After three failed attempts, the machine simply 'ate' his card and he was penniless in America. If there's a moral to the story it has to be: don't put all your eggs in one wallet. If you do, be sure you've got a back-up credit card or access to funds from other places. Commit your password to memory, and get it right the first time round.

Bring as much *moulla* to America as you like! But if you do bring along more than $10,000 in cash, you're asked to simply acknowledge you're carrying it on arrival. If you're toting heaps of cash and do not say so, you could be subject to forfeiting it all on the way in! I recommend you take $200 to $300 in small denominations to get you started, have those credit cards fully loaded and put some dosh into the ATM account to draw on as and when the mood for money moves you. That eliminates the need to carry wads of money about in America, where EVERYONE lives by the ATM and credit cards.

Just 'throw money at it!'

You only go around once, so make the most of it! Upgrade when and where it REALLY counts. Eat spaghetti, toss a few salads, or pan-fry a few bangers and mash with a side of mushy peas in the lead-up to your USA holiday so you can splurge where it really matters. Mix a night in a luxury suite in Las Vegas with a camping spot in Bryce Canyon. You'll remember the variety of options in America if you sample them fully.

Remember you'll find NY and LA street vendors flogging three T-shirts for $10 on Broadway and Sunset Strip. And enterprising fellows selling maps to the homes of Hollywood stars outside Mann's Chinese Theatre for $3.95. Equally, don't be surprised to see Navajo Indians selling $5000 woven rugs along the Arizona roadside or Texas-accented outfitters on Las Vegas street corners selling snakeskin boots. 'Shop till you drop!' will take on a newer, elevated meaning for you in America. And they all seem happy to take plastic! Be sure what you buy is not on an endangered list too.

Tipping in the States! Taxes too!

I had a first-timers table full of Australians out to a 'Dutch lunch' in Los Angeles many years ago, and when the bill was presented by our smiling, helpful-beyond-and-above-the-call-of-duty waitress and waiter, the Australians went into shock at the mere 'suggestion' of leaving a tip or gratuity. The very American idea of tipping wait staff, porters, bellhops, cabbies, and the like does take a bit of explaining. For some reason still unbeknown to this writer, waiters and waitresses in the USA are oftentimes paid below minimum wage, poverty-level hourly rates with the hope of making up the difference in tips. A 'tip' is given voluntarily by the consumer for providing excellent customer service. A tip has

America is a melting pot of cultures. Don't forget to tip!

never been compulsory, unless you're part of a large group. The great service you're given in the USA should be rewarded as a 'thank you' directly to your service provider as it is not factored into the cost of your meal. In hindsight, I think it's a good deal all around.

The portions and quality of meals in the USA tend to be significantly larger and less expensive than in other parts of the world, primarily due to the fact that the shopkeeper or owner has not had to load up labor costs in the price of putting the goods onto your table. We're confident you'll agree that the value is clearly there. And after your first real meal, you'll know why the Americans invented the take away 'doggie bag' for the remains of a great meal you simply couldn't possibly finish in one sitting. Here is the inside track on tipping with a few of our own time-tested tips:

- A tip is meant to be provided for excellent service. If you feel you've been slighted, just walking off will only make you the bad guy. If you feel your service provider did not live up to expectations, you can leave a smaller gratuity, or ask to speak with the management to let them know you were unhappy with the level of service and, therefore, not comfortable with leaving a tip when you go. You'll find that this is an extremely rare case, as your waiter or waitress is depending on great reviews and giving you top-shelf service in the hope of a nice tip on the tail end.

- Restaurant staff, waiters, and waitresses are those folks who actually bring food, take orders, provide service, clear plates, pour wine, and perform other duties, which make eating out a pleasure in the USA. Not required for the 'tipping thing' are fast food outlets, drive-thrus and other venues where you're expected to clear your own table, or order from the counter directly.

- The tip or gratuity for wait staff can usually be rounded up or down to the nearest dollar at 15%—with some folks tipping up to 20% in bigger cities like New York. Your tip should be calculated before any 'tax' that appears on the 'bill' or 'check'. Please smile, you've just had an excellent meal with more on the platter than you'd bargained for.

- Taxi drivers: Cabbies expect 15% to 20% of the fare, but I'm a firm believer in making them work for the extras. I ask questions, probe for information, and otherwise get them to spill the beans—my old man called it 'singing for your supper.'

- The limo driver: I'll gladly peel off a $5 or $10 note to pay my chauffeur. These private cars are becoming more and more prevalent as an option to taxi cabs and are my personal favorites. When you think of the bragging rights, and the door-to-door services they provide, it's a cheap ride really. In some cases, especially in and around major cities, I've been able to book a private limo for within $5 to $10 of a 'full-flag' fare on the meter of a regular cab. Plus, I get to sit back in the leather and surf the TV channels while the guy in the tie gets me there.

- The hotel and housekeeping staff: Many hotels now have a cute little card that sits below your fold-down chocolates, or the night table telling you the name of your maid or service provider. My simple method of saying thank you for the extra towels, shampoos, soap, and slippers is to slip a few dollars under the night-lamp when I leave—or a buck a day if I'm in one venue for a week or more.

- The front desk staff: The folks on reception who check

you in and tally your account at the end of your stay do not expect or require a tip. If I stay more than a week I bring a dozen donuts.

- The hotel or airport porter: If a porter touches your bag, it's generally a buck a bag. Three bags = $3 as a suggestion, excluding any of your own carry-on baggage. It's ok if you let the porter know from the very start that you're happy to handle your own items.
- The hairdresser, barber and hair stylist: Remember when you sit down in the chair to smile. These folks are working on you with sharp implements and will be expecting something in the range of 12% to 15% for giving you a totally new look.
- The long and short of tipping is that, as consumers, we still wind up out front when all is said and done. Just tote a pocketful of $1 bills to cover the tips.

⑥. Insurance, health, and safety —Don't leave home without it!

'Have a headache? Aspirin anyone?' That'll be $9.50 each tablet thanks, if it is administered in a hospital, anywhere in the USA. By comparison, the same $9.50 in any drug store or supermarket will buy you a massive bottle of aspirin, perhaps 300 capsules or more for your money. What gives?

If you're going to the States, you simply must have medical insurance! Medical attention in the USA is among the best in the world—however, you'll pay one arm, one leg, and other body parts to acquire it. Medical coverage is absolutely essential in America. Don't even think about leaving home without it. Take proof of coverage with you. In the event you need medical attention, one of the first questions on the paperwork for admittance will be, how you are intending to take care of the tab. It's the first thing on the paperwork after you write your surname. Ask your local travel guru about coverage, but shop around with your current insurance company. Premiums vary greatly, depending on age, pre-existing conditions, and length of stay so be sure to consider the options for the coverage that suits you best.

Medical necessities. If you're going to take your medications along to America, be sure the pharmacy labels are correct for prescriptions. If you need to carry injection needles, or blood sugar testing apparatus, ask your doctor or local pharmacist to provide a note to this effect. For any special prescriptions you may need filled while in the USA, you will more than likely need to see a 'GP' or general practitioner to secure a prescription that is recognized locally for refills. In some cases, the American Diabetes Association and others can be of help if needed. Research these collaborative relationships before leaving home, so you have toll-free numbers and contact details in case you need help while in America.

As for your toiletries, just tote along the bare necessities, because even these items are cheaper than chips in the States. For some good tips on what to pack and where to pack it, try www.travellerspoint.com.

Drug stores, some bigger than sporting stadiums, boast isle after isle of toothpastes, over-the-counter medications for 'what ails ya' and ailments you never even considered having until you began reading the labels. A drug store in the USA dispenses so much more than medicinal items. While inside some of these stores (if you ask for the nearest 'chemist' locals will think you've gone off the deep end), you can also land yourself fishing tackle, DVDs, magazines and books, ice chest, lawnmowers, cold beers, and even the occasional garden gnomes and gazebos. Or a 10-man camping tent.

It's always a good idea to keep your medications, inhalers etc along with the appropriate medical note from your friendly GP in the event you're asked to explain at the airport. If you're considering sneaking something which isn't quite acceptable (or legal) into the USA, DON'T! American Immigration and Customs officials have a zero tolerance for this type of activity. Zero.

7. Planning, public holidays, and online resources

I have always depended on the kindness of strangers.
Tennessee Williams

Let everyone know you're planning a trip to the USA. They'll have advice, stories in abundance, and recommendations of their own to share. Go online to 'human' venues, such as www. zuji.com.au, or www.travelocity.com, or www.holidaysonsale. com.au. Ask your local travel agent for brochures, maps, and advice and feel free to fire off a few questions to promotional organizations that encourage trade and travel to the USA. www. discoveramerica.com. Our own site is always open for queries at www.overeasyguides.com. Fire away! 'The journey of 1,000 miles begins with the first step.' Today, I think this needs to be amended to read: 'The journey of 1,000 miles begins with the first 'click' of the mouse.'

As you've by now already noted, this book is riddled with website contacts. For very good reasons. I'd like to lay down a few worldly words about the web. It's official: Americans have statistically turned the corner, booking more than 50% of their travel online. This means the web has taken over from previous and more traditional methods of booking travel and holiday planning. The rest of the planet is also headed here as an entire new generation only knows the internet as its way of linking to family, community, nation, and the world. 'Let your fingers do the walking' takes on new meaning and is being expanded to letting your fingers do the talking, the booking, the negotiation, and the discovery. And almost any other activity needed to create a trip to the USA. Questions so far? Ask www.wiki.answers.com.

When you invest in a holiday, expect to experience activities that are outside your daily routines and attitudes. Tour operators, adventure outfitters, visitors, convention bureaus, and motor-coach programs have been researching, honing, and delivering some fantastic itineraries in the USA for eons. Locking onto full-color brochures from your friendly travel agent can take you to places you'd never even considered, help you establish your own pace of night stops, and give you a solid foundation of places, activities, and even hotels to consider when making your own arrangements. And while you're poaching information and gleaning these seductive brochures of what's on offer, you might just find one that fits you perfectly.

Shopping around on the internet has revealed countless pages on places, reviews, and travel blogs by folks who've already been there and done that—pre-kicking the tires for you before you lift your own landing gears. Enjoy yourself.

Buy as much travel content as you can before leaving home. This way you know before you go what the bulk of your spending is going to be, and you'll not be in for any major surprises ... that is, until you begin packing your suitcases for the return trip home and discover your credit cards and luggage are both bursting at the seams.

When all your homework is done, I suggest booking the big bits with your local travel agent guru. I always like to hand over my hard-earned holiday money to a real person, so if I have any issues or changes to make, I can sit across the desk of a real person! Using a professional travel agent costs nothing more to accomplish and, if I have any issues, I know I have someone I can look to, instead of a website or having to navigate myself thru a lenthy phone-in system somewhere in another part of the planet.

Circumventing the queues and lines and saving time

If 'time is money', be sure to get yourselves one of those all-inclusive, mates' rates' passes for the places you want to explore. Look into pre-purchasing a CityPass™ product. They are the bees-knees because you save up to 50% or better, and more importantly, you cut the waiting time at pay booths, which gives you more time to explore and enjoy, and less time waiting in

Buy passes and bypass the lines—spend more time in the pool

lines. Look into www.citypass.com to find out more.

There are other pass cards on the market that use a credit card or swipe card type system, but I've found them to be too hard to decipher the distinctions, conditions, and inclusions. If you like having a credit card type option, look into 'Smart' or 'Go' Cards for the areas you plan to visit.

If you do get caught on a line or two, take full advantage of this opportunity to chat with the folks also in-waiting. I've said it all before, but the locals love your accent so plan to use it to full advantage, and remember, you're going away to America to see and do things you wouldn't otherwise be doing at home. So be adventurous and step out of yourself from time to time. You'll be very pleasantly surprised. I'm convinced one of the reasons long-haul visitors to the USA come back again and again is the Americans themselves. They are excellent hosts, love showing off their country, and they will go out of their way to enlighten, inspire, or educate when asked.

Check at the attraction or hotel about 'fast-track' or VIP tickets. You'll pay a bit more but you can often times get into places an hour before they open up to the general public, or you can discreetly cut the lines altogether. For a fellow who hates waiting around in line, I'm always happy to pay a bit more.

Public holidays and business hours

Americans love holiday celebrations and often take to the open road, the streets, parks, and public places in droves to make the most of these occasions. These holidays can put some pressure on visitors in terms of nailing down hire cars, lining up for attractions and events, and in some cases finding accommodations. Having said this, try to plan a trip that encompasses a major holiday event in America and celebrate alongside the Americans. Here are some of the nationally recognized 'public' holidays:

Christmas Day — December 25

New Years' Day — January 1

Memorial Day — May 30, signals the start of American 'summer'

Independence Day — July 4

Labor Day — first Monday in September, signals the end of American 'summer'

Columbus Day — second Monday in October

Presidents' Day — third Monday in February

Martin Luther King Jr Day. — third Monday in January

Veteran's Day — November 11

Thanksgiving Day — fourth Thursday in November

Easter Sunday — third Sunday in April

When visiting the USA, keep your eyes peeled for regional and 'unofficial' holidays as well. Halloween and 'trick or treating' on October 31 for example, is a major event date in America. Go ahead, grab a costume, and cash in on the lollies going from door to door.

Special interest groups often host annual events that attract attention: Ernest Hemingway days, Elvis events, 'Hug An Australian Week', and others are all worthy of consideration. If you're keen to research into the historical significance of American holidays try online at www.wikipedia.org and simply search 'Public Holidays USA'.

In general, most American shopping malls open their doors to the public at 10am, and many stay open 'till late'. Other businesses, libraries, post offices, banks, and public buildings generally open from 9am until 5pm Mondays through Fridays.

The USA is a melting pot

8. Embassies, consulates, and tourist offices

There are two very powerful schools of thought on 'staying in touch' while on a visit to the USA. One way of thinking is to simply cut all ties and communications with the home-front while you're away, while the other point of view is to have at the ready, ways of keeping constant vigilance on the pets, kids, home, and the office from afar.

Many international visitors simply make alterations to their mobile network so it works in the USA, others buy a 'toss away' phone' while traveling to stay in touch, confirm reservations, or call road service. Last, but in no way suggested to be the least, go underground. Nobody finds you unless it is really really really important.

One thing to do in the unlikely event of an emergency is to dial 911 to have direct access to an emergency operator in your area. This line is not to be used lightly because all calls are recorded and used to report emergencies for fire, police, and medical services.

Another toll-free line has recently been established for directory assistance locally, and medical emergencies and can be accessed by simply dialing 411.

Finally, another less demanding contact while in the USA is with the Travelers' Aid Society', which maintains 24-hour hotlines for help. It's a toll-free call on 1-800-327-2700 and the society can also be contacted on www.travelersaid.com.

In the event of an emergency call:

911 for all emergencies, anywhere in America.
411 for directory assistance
1-800-327-2700 for Travelers' Aid

You should always have, in your possession, contact details for your home embassy or consul-general. For example:

Australia – www.austemb.org
New Zealand – www.nzembassy.com
South Africa – www.saembassy.org
United Kingdom – www.britainusa.com

Before leaving home, it's a very good idea to photocopy a leave-behind list and a carry-on list of your passport, credit cards, insurance details, equipment ID numbers, and other valuables.

You may never need it but a 'crib sheet' of these details could save you heaps of time, frustration, and money. Stow them in your luggage separately.

Once in the USA, great sources of fliers, maps, and other complimentary materials can be spotted and tapped. The hotel lobby and concierge's desk, airport visitor information counter, visitors and convention centers, and public areas and attractions have promotional fliers, brochures, and timetables for things to do locally.

When on the road, especially when entering a new state, there will be a signpost on most interstate highways for a 'Tourist & Visitors' Information Center. These are combined with state-run and funded rest rooms and rest (picnic) areas.

Of the 50 states that comprise the USA, each has a toll-free telephone number with recorded messages and you can speak with a tourism specialist on that number for specific help and information. Collecting brochures of places, events, national parks, and attractions you've visited make lasting mementos of any visit. Take only the collaterals you think you'll need, because most of America is trying to think of ways to prevent cutting down trees. I've witnessed hoards of small children fill shopping bags with this creative collateral, only to have a parent tip the entire ensemble into the bin. Take what you need and leave the rest for the next person.

Toll-free calling for visitors is significant, so plan to make the most of it. By simply dialing 1-800-555-1212 you can ask for a toll free number for hotels, attractions, visitors and convention bureaus, travel insurance providers, national parks, campgrounds, state tourism entities, and thousands of other sources, and you won't need to feed the phone. Every credit card company will have a 24/7 toll-free contact number in the USA, in the event you need to report a card as lost or stolen, or organize a replacement while in the USA. If your intended phone number begins with either '800', '877', '866' or '888' it's 'on the house' and toll free to you while in the USA.

Phone cards, which allow you to make national and international calls, are available almost anywhere, especially at corner stores. Pick the one that best suits your needs, as they vary widely. You can always phone home collect from any phone booth or hotel, but this will be at a significantly higher rate. It's always a good idea to ask the front desk first about charges for outside calls to avoid shocks to the wallet when checking out.

Many visitors to the USA now buy a phone, and load it with minutes to use while on holiday. You can then use this phone to confirm arrival times, make reservations, get directions and more as a 'local' call, saving heaps of roaming charges and home-country additional fees. Be careful if you use your own mobile with roaming charges, which can mount up quickly.

A final few word on phones. The Americans say each and every number in consecutive order, so they'll be totally befuddled if you use your 'double six, triple five, naught' lingo on them. 'Naught' or 'zed' at home is a 'zero' in America. Try it anyhow, just to see the reaction as it's good for a laugh.

⑨. Post, communications, and internet

US post offices are open from 9am until 5pm daily, Monday though Friday, with many now also open on Saturday mornings. Post offices dispense stamps, stationery, mailing containers and take in mail and parcels as their core business. You can also plan to have your mail kept at a specific post office as 'general delivery' if you know the five-digit zip code (www.zip4. usps.com) or the postal code of the specific post office. Most post offices will 'hold' general delivery' letters for 30 days before

Drop us a postcard please—we'd love to hear from you!

'return to sender' kicks in, and a small fee is charged if you wish to have mail forwarded. Ask for specifics from the US Postal Service at www.usps.com. Street-side postboxes in the USA are prevalent and always deep blue in color.

10. TV, radio, books, newspapers, and magazines

By asking around at the front desk, engaging the locals, reading the daily newspapers, and tuning into the local radio DJs, you'll learn lots. You'll discover an antique show, the organic market, a 'white elephant' sale, a classic car show, a high school sporting event, outdoor free film festivals, and a host of other great local activities. Tune in for community celebrations, such as parades, fish fests or pig roasts, chili cook-offs, local rodeos, and countless other offerings that you can simply tag along to.

TV and radio

America has a harvest of abundant local and regional TV and radio stations, and the hardest part is finding the ones you want to follow. Most hotels now are plugged into national cable programming so prepare yourself for channel-surfing syndrome if you're not careful. In my opinion, about 80% of the offerings on air are *garbone* (garbage in Italian). When our troops travel together, the TV simply stays switched off. Jump in the pool, kick a ball around, go for a hike—anything reasonable is better than sitting in front of the box.

Radio stations across America tend to be very specific in speaking to their audience demographic, and channel surfing will bring you all types of information on a more local level. Before going, plug your listening preferences into a web-based search engine for radio stations in the areas you'll be visiting. Print out the list and you're all set to start monkeying with the tuning dials on your own radio. www.radio-locator.com is a place to get started. These folks have listed stations by state and interest as well.

Ipods are both a good and a bad idea. They can keep kids occupied for long stretches, but the downside is they totally eliminate any possibility of a two-sided conversation—unless you know signing and sign-language. As a general rule, we've suggested to our flock that using the ipods is fine while in-flight, or on long stretches of open highway in between points of interest—otherwise they stay switched off and safely tucked away.

Books, newspapers, and magazines

Newsstands, corner stationeries, and chain bookstores are abundant in the USA. Local libraries, although not keen to lend books to out-of-towners, are safe havens with soft seats, clean desks, and plenty of light to catch up on the local news, browse national magazines, or to check on reference books related to travel. Almost all American libraries are now connected to the internet so you can check your emails and search as you please. Some charge a minimal fee for the service if you don't hold a local library card. Ask the librarian for help. Internet cafes and coffee shops have also made it possible to 'hook-up' almost anywhere.

Many larger bookstore chains have recently adopted a library template, where you can grab a cup of Starbucks coffee, and peruse the books and magazines on offer—a sort of 'kick the tires first' proposition, which many overseas visitors use to full advantage while traveling.

I've never-ever gone to the States without bringing back books. It's my thing. I've uncovered everything from a first edition Ernest Hemmingway to a signed copy of Truman Capotes' *In Cold Blood* and Yevi Yevtashenkos' signature in a St. Vincent de Paul store. But oftentimes local community clubs do not-for-profit book fairs and book swaps, and other book venders offer up 'seconds' or 'remainders' at prices I just can't get past. Our kids collect comic books, some of which are suitable for trading. I like the idea of recycling. Many 'Ma and Pa' eateries, campgrounds, truck stops, and motor inns offer up swap-a-book shelves, which make it easy to take one and leave one behind. You'll find swap-a-book shelves salt and peppered all across America. Try your luck at a local swap meet—you'll be amazed at what the Americans are trying to clear out of the attic, at often unbelievable bargains.

11. Photography, video, and your journal

Capture and record everything! You never know when you're going to go back! Through technology, it's now within the general population's power to snap away and successfully get some great shots in the bag. I'm a walking advert for these new-

Happy snaps and journals allow you to revisit as often as you like

fangled, and easy to use 'idiot proof' cameras and recording devices.

Feel free to share. With the internet, the world has shrunk significantly, and blogs, websites, amateur reviewers sites, personal domains, and others have provided a stage for sharing travel-related experiences with a much broader audience than just our neighbors over the fence. In some cases, your images and word-smithing can even help pay the way. News editors, programming directors, and tourism entities could all be potential buyers of your creative juices, so snap away.

Online sites, such as www.zuji.com.au and www.travelocity. com, post regular submissions and often run competitions but hundreds of places on the web want your stuff.

Get into the habit of keeping a journal. Just a few lines each day for reminiscing in your old age. Diaries and journals have a way of allowing time travel. A few words that you write during your trip will allow you to become a time traveler in much the

Capture the moments

same way an old song, a scent, or an old photograph can be. I've taken to writing postcards to myself, which I then compile into a sort of scrapbook of trips, but there are thousands of variations on this theme. Go to www.scrapbookscrapbook.com for some insider trading on the subject.

The possibilities for capturing funny road signs, quirks in American menus, singular sayings that caught your attention, or simply the mileage, temperature, and frame of mind you were in on any given day can all add to the emotional and memorable scrapbook.

12. Weights and measures, temperatures and electricity

Despite the fact that the USA 'officially' adopted the metric system over 30 years ago, the country still measures in miles, inches, feet, quarts, and gallons, much to the amazement of the rest of the planet. The most frequently used and confused conversions take place when shopping. For example, when you buy your gasoline or gas in the USA, you'll be buying it by the 'gallon' which converts to 3.79 liters. A handy place to look is www.onlineconversion.com where they convert just about anything for you, and some things you never even thought of converting.

If you're buying Maine lobster (crayfish) or Devon (Bologna) by the pound (lb.) you're actually at .45 of a kilo. When the road sign says you're in the desert with only 1 mile to go to the next watering hole, you'll be driving or pushing the car 1.61 kilometers. A full list of conversions is available at the back of this book, and we'd love to hear any of your stories about the conversion process on www.overeasyguides.com.

Converting verbal directions from an American can be challenging. If you ask a midwesterner how far to the next gas station, he or she might just say with a smile, 'Oh, it's only just down the road apiece' which in translation can be anything from one to 100 miles off. So try to home in a bit better when getting the help from the locals.

Electricity in the USA is based on a 110-volt, two or three (the ground plug is often round) prong system that means that most of the rest of the world, on 220 or 240 volts, will be underpowered if you plug your home country item in without an adapter. Exceptions to this rule do apply; for example, in most major hotels, the bathroom electrical socket may well accommodate your shaver or hair-dryer. But it's safe to check first with the appliance to see if it can be converted to use in the USA by the simple flick of a switch. Campgrounds are another exception, and most American RVs and boats that require 'shore-power' run on 220-volt systems.

As a general rule, always check first before plugging in, and when in doubt ask someone at the front desk or reception. The wall switches in America are in the down position when they are on, and in the up position when they are off and wall 'sockets' do not have individual on-off switches. If you do blow a fuse, you'll oftentimes take the neighbors down with you until someone locates the 'circuit-breaker box'. Don't panic however, it rarely happens, and if you're the cause of the electrical disturbance, simply look skyward and act innocent of all charges.

Temperature measurement is another oddity of Americans; so don't panic when you hear those incredibly high temperatures from the local weatherman. America is on the Fahrenheit system when it appears most of the world operates on the Centigrade formula. What it means is that when the newscaster suggests the temperature is going to drop to 32 degrees Fahrenheit, it's the temperature at which water freezes. In winter time, cold weather temperatures are also calculated with the addition of a formula for the 'wind chill factor', which can take a cold day on the ski slopes and turn it even colder by the time the wind-whip is taken into consideration. Finally, all external temperatures are measured 'in the shade' so when they remind you it's going to be 120 degrees in Death Valley, that's hot. We've included at the back of the book a temperature chart. It converts from Fahrenheit to Centigrade for your enlightenment and edification. Dress or undress accordingly.

Buying clothes and shoes in the USA is a fantastic pastime,

once you get over the sizing shenanigans of the Americans. My motto is 'try everything on'. Test it out in front of the mirror. Ask complete strangers how you look. Then make a purchase. Sales staff are mostly very friendly. Some even have a vested interest (commission) in making sure you're looking good.

If you're buying clothing items for a friend, be sure of the sizes before buying. Returns and exchanges may be difficult, if not prohibitive, from thousands of miles away. There are at the time of writing, at least three world-recognized sizing formulas; Continental, American, and British, and the variation from one to the other can be extreme.

Dress accordingly. If you don't own it yet, buy it in the USA.

13. Shopping in America

Overseas visitors to the States continue to rank 'shopping' as the number one activity they enjoy while visiting. It is no longer just those running shoes and blue jeans that are getting scooped up at pleasing prices. I've seen everything from golf clubs, sporting equipment, camping tents, barbeque grills, fishing gear, electric guitars, computers, laptops, lawn mowers and more make their way to the check-in line at the airport.

If you grab a real bargain, be prepared to pay the duty on it, if asked. Check on the customs allowances beforehand, so you're not unpleasantly surprised when you tote your newly acquired goodies home. I pack my new purchases and receipts together to provide proof to the customs officer on arrival. I declare everything, and in most cases the duty officer simply waves me through after looking my items over. Breaking in those fantastic $8 blue jeans I bought at Wal-Mart before heading home means they're now well worn in, as well as 'used'. I do the same thing with my new shoes.

My kids love the breakfast cereals they make in the USA, possibly because they're loaded with sugar and marshmallows and other items we don't normally see at our breakfast table. Check on food items that are permissible. If you plan to bring food of any kind into or out of the country, be certain the packaging remains fully sealed. There are no guarantees your item of food will be allowed through customs, so I suggest you don't go overboard purchasing heaps of it.

A few words of caution when buying items in the USA. If you're buying an item that requires electrical power, be sure it has a switch for converting to your home country's voltage. Otherwise you'll be spending money on a 'converter' to power your new purchase.

Plastic is accepted almost everywhere. 'Have a nice day!'

Garage sales, yard sales, white elephant sales, weekend markets, St. Vincent de Paul stores, and other not-for-profit places are brilliant spots to hunt for bargains. I'm a scavenger and proud of it. Old and out-of-print books, fishing rods and reels, old watches, and more are my usual prey but I love a bargain of any type. You'll locate these venues by simply asking around, or picking up the local newspaper. Be prepared to haggle with the seller, but no need to get mean about it. Nine out of ten times you'll grab a real steal and make an acquaintance in the same transaction. Quality clothing and kids' toys are often cheaper than a bag of chips. Americans always buy more than they can use so grabbing a pre-owned item gets goods out of their attics and into circulation again.

Shopping rules, indoors, outdoors or in between

Dynamic 'drug stores' with much, much more!

The corner drug store and high-stool 'soda fountain' of yesteryear America are few enough to be counted on your 10 toes. Mega-drug marts and mall drug stores, seeming to sell, well, everything, have replaced them.

Visiting an American 'drug store' is a must. You can grab everything from garden tools and circus-sized backyard tents to watches, magazines and books, cold drinks, alcoholic beverages, and much more in these relatively new additions to the American shopper's landscape. Not to mention the items they sell for your health, personal hygiene, prescription drugs, and bodybuilding.

Specialty Shops. If you can buy it, Americans will have a retailer whose business it is to sell it to you. Specialty shops for surf wear, fitness, ladies, men's, and kids clothing, 'Big' men and women's sizes, western wear, firearms, photography, sports memorabilia, stamp and coin collecting, adult toys, and any other item you can possibly imagine will have a shop-specific to that product or service.

Just look at the size of the yellow pages phonebook in your hotel desk drawer or night table if you need proof. Many of these shops are located along the main street, or at strip malls or as in-line tenants in bigger shopping centers or shopping malls.

Mega Malls. I'm waiting for the day when some bright spark develops a global navigation device for use in the mega mall. I always get lost. I wish I'd bought along a homing pigeon when trying to navigate myself back to my parked car. But once inside, these venues offer more than just shopping. Many have amusement park rides and attractions, multi-screen movie theaters, and more. Restaurants, pubs, food courts, energy drink concessions, and confectionary specialists all help to keep our tank topped up from shop to shop.

Shopping is the number one preferred activity for overseas visitors

I have two hard-and-fast rules I adhere to before attempting the mega mall. First, I make a detailed note of where I've parked my vehicle, noting my license plate number so when I can't find it after an hour long siege of the lot, I can provide the parking lot security team with details. Second, I become a man with a mission. I penetrate the interior of the mall with a specific goal in mind; underwear and socks, a high-tech camping tent or sleeping bag, clothing gifts for my wife and kids that's 'cool', or some other single-minded spend. Once this task is accomplished I can relax, look around, and get lost a few more times before attempting the long trek back to find my car. If you want to pre-plan your own mall invasion, try www.shopamericatours.com.

The mother lode of all malls in America has got to be the Mall of America in Minnesota. With over 40 million visitors a year, the joint is the size of seven Yankee Stadiums and covers over 4.2

million square feet of space. Even if you never get there, you need to see what all the fuss is about. Go to www.mallofamerica.com and ride the simulated roller coasters from the lobby.

The department stores and 'anchor' tenants. Of all the department stores we tear through while visiting the USA, Macys takes the cake for looking after international visitors. Arm yourself and your entire crew with a free, International shoppers' discount card and you're away on some of the best bargains ever. The discount card currently offers an additional 11% off purchases, and this includes items that are already on sale. So if Macys is doing a 75% off sale on clothing, I get to take off an additional 11%, that means my shopping cart runneth over with purchases. To get your discount card, simply ask. Be willing to show your passport and air ticket. Try www.macys.com to get a head start on the shopping.

14. Eat out! Eat up!

Our culture runs on coffee and gasoline,
the first often tasting like the second.
Edward Abbey, author

When America first took to the open road in cars, not much of it was paved. Gas stations, rest areas, and visitors' centers were only a twinkle in a road planner's eye. This led to a lot of 'greasy spoon' venues serving up questionable eats to passers-by. Belly-aching was par for the course. So many of America's earlier road travelers began seeking out the truck stops, diners, and take-away venues that long-haul drivers frequented. The rationale was that if those guys were stopping off, the home-made apple pie and fresh brewed coffee would be ok. Food

All roads lead to good eats

quality and content was all over the shop until a very clever hotel owner named Howard Johnson standardized the food that was served in his venues. He even showed in photographs on his menus, exactly what your BLT and fries was going to look like, right down to the pickle wedge on the side, resting comfortable on a piece of lettuce. He also made sure the roadside billboards let passers-by know the toilet was clean as a whistle. Americans filled his Howard Johnsons' Motor Inns, safely parking the family wagon in front of their rented rooms' front door and ate his well-photographed burgers. He later added pools and TVs and the rest is history.

Ask Around in America. More than likely you'll find out from the locals what their specialty is. When you're in New Orleans, you've got to try the Creole and Cajun spicy foods including the gumbo and jambalaya. Wash them down with a few high-octane Hurricane cocktails. If you're in the New England states, the lobster, 'Cherrystone clams' and New England clam chowder (it's the one with the white sauce as compared to 'Manhattan clam chowder', which is in a tomato based or red sauce) are the go. Major cities across the USA have specialty steak houses (specifically, the Midwest is well known for its beef) where the meat is aged and magnificent. Trust us. You'll be asking for a doggie bag as portions in these places tend to be mammoth as well as mouth-watering. In the Deep South, it's Bar B Q Ribs, grits, and buffalo wings with spices. In some cities, the town stakes its reputation on a particular specialty, like a Philadelphia cheesesteak or a 'hoagie' sandwich. Anywhere in the Midwest, you've got miles and miles of sweet corn, and potatoes that occasionally come in the size of a good soccer ball—we've not seen a bigger potato anywhere that can top the Idaho spuds. Atlanta, Georgia boasts about its country fried steaks and mint juleps. Along the American coastline comes the 'catch of the day'. New York's street vendors hawk chorizo sausages, Coney Island hot dogs with all the trimmings, roasted chestnuts, and plentiful toasted pretzels. The Big Apple in fact, hosts an annual 'Vendys Award' for the best street vendors' food

Ask for a 'doggie bag'—the portions are monumental.

Don't expect to lose weight in the States—everything is super-sized!

on offer so it pays to eat at the curb occasionally.

A new guidebook suggests you eat all your meals from street vendors in the major American cities. Coastal venues are a shoe-in for seafood specials and the catch-of-the-day culinary delights. Soft-shelled crab from Chesapeake Bay, Cherrystone clams from the Cape, lobsters from Maine, and abalone from Big Sur. Hungry yet?

Try the deli sandwiches in the States, the size is enormous by our standards. Delis, corner groceries, and supermarket delicatessen sections all seem to produce a 'super-sized' sandwich with exactly what you like on it for cheap. Save the uneaten half for later. Or share with a friend. Many major supermarket chains now also offer loyal shoppers' cards, which you can swipe every time you shop and save. Just ask for yours at the cash register.

Street eats. Try the Coney Island hot dogs with 'the works'.

THE WHEEL
AMERICA

TAKING TO THE OPEN ROAD

1. On the road travel tips

An American author, William 'Least Heat' Moon penned a book entitled *Blue Highways* about 30 years ago. It's an excellent read. I've included it in your reading list for later. Old Least Heat, a native American, was feeling the heat of a rocky relationship and lit out like other writers before him, such as John Steinbeck and Jack Kerouac. They discovered the real America by taking those little varicose-vein roads between places, while avoiding the big American super-slabs, highways, and mega freeways. Their books are more about the people they rubbed elbows with en route. They really only scratched the surface of road trip possibilities. Go for it!

If it's got wheels and goes, Americans will rent it to you

Americans love taking to the open road and why not?! There are over 7.4 million miles of it (and that's just the black-topped ones). Driving for overseas visitors is a cinch if you keep a couple of critical bits of information in mind when settling yourself behind the wheel for your road trip.

Attitude is 95% of driving enjoyably in America. So if you get lost, celebrate the opportunities and maintain calm in the car. A simple tip that most Americans still don't know is that every major roadway in the USA has a number that tells you in what direction it travels for the most part. Grab the map of the USA and you'll spot it right away: All of the major interstate highways that run in an east to west direction have one thing in common: they have EVEN numbers, and conversely, all major interstate highways that run north to south are all given ODD numbers.

This is the reason the famed 'Highway 66' was dismantled. It spent half its life going south and north and the other half headed west or east. When you look at your national map, you'll make another enlightened discovery. Route 95 runs the entire eastern seaboard of the USA, while Highway 1 snakes its way along the entire West Coast of America. Major interstate loop roads that help you skirt around major metropolitan areas at rush hour usually have 3-digit numbers. So around Washington DC, you could have the 195 which is closer in to the Capital than the 295 the 395, or the 495 if that helps.

Study the map before you leave the parking lot, then drive off to get lost in the USA. Everyone else does it. An intelligent investment in your holiday on the road is a Rand McNally Road Atlas available at any supermarket, drugstore, or mega shop, as well as most gas stations (petrol stations).

Just follow the signs and you won't get lost. It's easy!

Driving tips

Before you even put the key in the car, adjust your mirrors, seats, and headrests, then clip in your seat belts.

First, Americans drive on the wrong side of the road. It's totally left-hand drive unless you're going to rent a garbage truck with duel controls. Americans drive on the right side of the road.

When in doubt, simply follow the vehicle in front of you. It doesn't take very long to figure this one out, especially if you try to enter the on-ramp of an LA freeway going in the wrong direction. Plenty of locals will flick you a hand sign (middle finger solo) or arm gesture (commonly referred to as up yours!), or more commonly done, flash their headlights and lean on their horns to enlighten you of your directional error. If you want to brush up on driving rules and regulations, road signs and distances, try www.usatourist.com.

I suggest you don't step off your plane and step directly behind the wheel of your American rental. It's far better to rest up a day and get acclimatized to looking in the other direction when stepping off the curb. Then when you have a little better lay of the roadway, strike out for the open road.

Seatbelts save lives, and throughout America you'll see billboards, roadside reminders, and bumper stickers to remind

Remember Americans drive on the 'wrong side' of the road

you of this fact. It's the law. Although individual states may post different requirements and restrictions, to stay on the safe side of the law, simply buckle up and you're covered, full stop. Some states have specific requirements for car seats and little ones, and strong warnings about infants in front seats that are equipped with airbags. Check these before driving away from your rental car lot or pick-up depot.

This brings us to another item of interest. A FULL STOP sign in America is an eight-sided, shocking-red sign that means exactly what the word STOP in its center suggests. Unlike other countries, Americans insist on a full stop that means, 'breaking the full forward momentum of the vehicle' and then checking before advancing. Rolling through or simply tapping the brake pedal lightly at a STOP sign will attract state troopers like moths to the flame, and they'll be happy to point out the 'finer' points of the law as they 'write you up'.

In every state of the USA, the pedestrian has the right of way. He should not be seen by drivers as a moving target. Remember too that you'll be driving on the wrong side of the roadway so pedestrians may appear from the curb when you least expect them.

According to the AAA (American Automobile Association), most states acknowledge the drivers' licenses and credentials of other countries for visitors. This outfit also provides great driving tips for all seasons and although it is a member based organization, many of the materials and maps are available for the asking. Try www.aaa.com. If your license is not in English, you'll be required to get yourself an international drivers' license.

If you're taking to the road in a rented motor home or Harley Davidson 'hog', check with the rental outfit beforehand to be sure your particular paperwork is in order. Wearing helmets on motorcycles in our view is a must, but some states are laid back on this rule because of lobbying with local lawmakers. So before leaving home, it's a good idea to check on the particulars of what you need.

School crossings and school buses are almost always parakeet and banana yellow. They are very easy to spot. In EVERY state, if a school bus has its flashing lights in operation, vehicles in BOTH directions must come to a complete stop until after the STOP signs are turned off. This is very important as school children cross traffic directly in front of their school bus instead of waiting for the bus driver to pull away from the curb. Penalties for these infractions are very serious and violators are heavily fined by local judges.

Useful tools on the road

For around US$100 you can hook-up your very own CB (Citizen Band) radio, which will provide hours of roadway banter between yourself and other road warriors. Go on; give yourself a 'handle' so you can chat up the over-the-road and long-haul big rig drivers. They'll love your accent; and perhaps offer proposals of marriage or pancakes with eggs over easy. Other countries have restrictions on the importation of the CB radios because they also feature the police and emergency frequencies. So check at home before attempting to bring yours home with you.

CB roadway banter is excellent for picking up the road conditions for the miles in front of you, tipping off the location of rolling 'smokies' (speed cameras and radar guns are almost entirely hand operated or car mounted by police) or picking out an occasional 'bear in the air' with police monitoring speeds from a light aircraft overhead or indicating 'fuzz-busters' (aka radar detectors). After my second speeding ticket in a week, I invested in a radar detector. I felt it was only fair, given the two tickets that 'drove' me to adopt my own counter intelligence

If you are lost, simply pull over and ask a local

were given for speeds under 40 miles an hour. I shelled out a little over $100 for the detector, which plugs into the cigarette lighter and sits peacefully on the dashboard until it goes off like rapid small gunfire as the police car approaches. Honestly, I'd have been happy to go through life without a detector, but without an intervention the odds were not in my favor.

Roadway signage in the USA makes it easy. Following those glow-in-the-headlamp signs can sometimes create challenges, or as my wife likes to call them, opportunities. Since they are plentiful, you may need to either slow down some to take note, or enroll in a speed-reading course when making full use of the US freeway and highway systems, especially in and around big cities.

Honestly, driving in the USA is easy. Rental companies, especially in major gateway cities, have a vast variety of wheels on offer. You're bound to find the road warrior that suits your needs to a tee. Convertibles, 4WD, motor-homes with all the creature comforts, people pleasers (people movers), even motorcycles of all descriptions are on offer if you hold the right credit card and credentials.

Renting vehicles

Try whenever renting to get the following value-added items included in the cost beforehand: 'Collision damage waiver' and 'unlimited mileage' are important. It's always a requirement that you have in your possession a valid driver's license from home and a credit card to cover any unexpected dings or bings. Renting a vehicle in the USA without these two items is near on impossible; so don't even go there.

Some hire firms have age restrictions, making would-be road warriors pay a higher rental rate if you are under the age of 21 or in some states, 25 years of age. Shopping around for the car you want at a price you'll be pleased with takes a bit of homework. You'll ultimately get what you're looking for if you dig around long enough.

In recent years, some companies have taken to 'renting wrecks' or older model cars that don't require high costs to replace. Yes, these seasoned road warriors can be a bargain if you're not traveling too far and not fussed or afraid to add water to an ailing radiator while crossing Death Valley. These outfits often cater to under 25-year-old drivers who might have age issues or restrictions with the major rental companies. A word of warning here. Unless your rental agreement allows it, do not take your car across the border into either Mexico or Canada. Especially Mexico!

America is the home of deals on wheels

Navigation

An American would rather give you the wrong directions,
than to have you think ill of them when you drove on.
Jake Brown, Boston merchant banker

It's somewhat sad to see the overwhelming takeover by GPS (Global Positioning Systems). They are those inside car navigators that will take you from point A to point B without ever having to roll the window down to ask a local. On the plus side of the ledger, GPS systems have dramatically reduced domestic squabbles, with the ability to 'tell you where to go!' in four or five, even six different languages. The upside is all those saved relationships. You won't miss the hours of pent up silence while trying to find the hotel or attraction that looked so attractive when you picked it out of the brochure or on the internet. You can simply flick a switch to turn off the instruction at leisure.

The downside of always knowing where you're going is that it eliminates the opportunity to engage the locals. Pulling to the curb to ask for directions, or asking the locals from atop a diner's stool can be extremely rewarding. Discuss renting the directional devices with your travel companion. After all, it's most often the co-pilot who gets stuck reviewing the road map, and spending significant time buried in the bowels of the latest road atlas to get you where you're trying to go.

With the GPS technology in tow, even the navigator can be looking at the scenery, and reminding you that you're going the wrong way on a one-way street instead of relying on the back seat occupants to chime in with these updates all the time. If you're looking for ideas on awesome road warrior itineraries to try, fasten your seat belt and put the pedal down to the metal to www.roadtripamerica.com. If you do have a GPS along, fake being lost from time to time and ask the locals.

Pick your pleasure

You can hire nearly any type of transport you please in the USA from tandem bicycles and electric scooters to luxury motor homes and Hummers, and everything in between. Harley Davidson motorcycles and other two-wheeled road warriors are available for the asking, but may require a hometown license to rent one. Eagle Rider is my favorite source of 'hogs' as they have depots nationwide. Try www.eaglerider.com. Prestige cars such as Cadillacs and Lincolns, sports cars, gas-guzzlers, environmentally friendly hybrids, and soft tops (convertibles) are easily acquired from most of the major car hire companies. I like the counter folks and the cars at Alamo. Try www.alamo.com. For recreational vehicles, I'm sold on the folks of El Monte on www.elmonterv.com.

When shopping for the best deals on wheels, first ask what it costs to get upgraded to a better model. Ask hire outfits to include in the price, 'unlimited mileage' costs instead of a set mileage distance fee that is bumped up later if you go over and beyond that distance. Also ask about including the 'collision damage waiver' (something similar to third party insurance) in the quote.

Gassing up

There is a gas station on the outskirts of Las Vegas, Nevada which goes where no other petrol-pumping publican dares to venture. A huge billboard out in front of the place stakes its claim clearly, even if the paint is now peeling under the onslaught of 100-degree heat: 'Friendly Advice Free Aspirin with every tank full. Our toilets don't bite!' Mind you, they charge $2 for bottled water and they are in the middle of the Nevada desert.

Gone are the days of an acne-covered kid flying from the office, starched uniform tucked neatly into his waistcoat, checking your oil. 'Can I top up the water?' is a phrase which has now gone the way of the dinosaur. When I was growing up, we simply sat in the car with our parents, while the attendant pumped gasoline costing 21 cents a gallon into the tank as we fondled the Bakelite plastic buttons on the AM radio. To quote my good buddy Michel Bouskila, those days are 'Gone, Gone, Gone!'

Almost all of America is do-it-yourself nowadays, and in some venues you never have to see the service (I think they should in fact rename these places cause it's downright misleading) station attendant. You insert your credit card, insert the nozzle, insert the gas, and you're gone again. Before car manufacturers put those little plastic connectors like 'idiot mittens' on the gas cap, millions of Americans drobe off without them.

On the bright side of things, 'gasoline' is still measured out in 'gallons' in America, as opposed to liters. Americans are the biggest consumers of petrol on the planet, a fact that has kept costs of distilling and distribution down and the production of bigger gas-guzzlers up. Things are changing, albeit slowly with issues of air pollution, global warming, and more awareness by the average American that he lives in a global village. You'll still get whiplash trying to tally up the number of huge Hummers and gas-guzzling giants that Americans 'just have to have'. For up-to-date fuel costs, based on each state go to www.fueleconomy.gov.

2. Air travel

After spending many years at 35,000 feet, I've developed some time-tested tips for making the most of the most popular way of getting to the USA.

Hunting for a fantastic airfare to America takes time, and once you've got the right flights, the best price, and your stars are all aeronautically in order, book it! Because more than likely, it won't be there tomorrow.

Once your flights are nailed down, the real maneuvering begins. I first make sure to check in on the fast-track lines afforded to frequent flier members. If I'm not a current member of that airline, I'll sign up because it's almost always free to begin. I hate waiting in long lines, and I've worked this magic successfully for over 30 years.

The other thing I work out in advance is pre-seating—selecting the place on the plane that best suits my family and me. I always insist on an aisle seat, so I can pop up and down like a yo-yo without confronting someone trying to watch the movie or sleep their way across the pond. I check on the 'type' of aircraft I'll be flying on, so I can determine if the entertainment is in the seat back, or can be rented as a hands-free item, or if the screens are a permanent fixture to the forward bulkheads. I also like to select my seats based on the fact that I'm not nested right alongside the galley where the crew drums up the rolling meal and beverage trays, or outside the toilet doorway. A website that promises the inside-skinny on finding the best seat is www. seatguru.com so peek at some of their tips and then take flight on your own seat selection.

I always travel with my blackout eye covers because I don't care if the person next to me is keen to read *War and Peace* in one sitting with their lights on throughout the flight. The other item I never leave home without is that u-shaped neck brace to prevent whiplash as I slip into slumber. I know, they look totally idiotic, but nobody on board will really see it once the cabin lights have been dimmed, and they make a monumental difference.

Sit back, relax and enjoy the ride—you're headed to the USA

It's a good idea to pre-order 'kids' meals and 'vegetarian' selections. These are always served first off so there is no waiting for the rolling carts to get to us. We're assured of our 'preference' and selection. In many cases, being at the rear of the aircraft means you might not have the menu selection you want because your choices are simply all gone.

It's ok to call your airline and ask about the 'load factor' for that flight. If the flight is lightly loaded, I get to the airport early, requesting an entire row of seats down the back. With the armrests up across the entire row, I've got myself a really comfy bed to sleep on.

There are a few things they never tell you until it's too late. For example, on many aircraft the bulkhead seats may have an inch or two more leg room, however the armrests will not lift. I've discovered this the hard way when I grabbed 'an entire row to myself' on a long-haul flight thinking I could stretch out, only to discover after take-off that the armrests weren't going anywhere. Another place that long-haul travelers target are the exit isles where more leg room is taken for granted. Although this is true, many of these seats are also loitering places for other passengers who roam the cabin during the flight so you may be under the microscope of public scrutiny, or have the lights from nearby toilets and the galley to contend with.

Security blankets. I've come to find comfort in the new, improved security screenings. The folks who are administering these necessary checks are, in large part, making my trip far more enjoyable, so I smile, assume I'm going to be shedding my shoes and belt and taking my laptop out of its leather nest and a number of other must-comply-if-I-want-to fly procedures. I've long ago given up thinking that the security teams are singling me out, or have taken their tasks of sifting through my dirty jockey shorts as part of a personal fetish.

To make it all run smooth as silk, my rule is simply to leave myself plenty of time for check-in, customs, immigration, and the protocols of travel in today's world. As security regulations change without notice, it is always a good idea to check close to your departure date. The Transportation Security Administration maintains a great site. Try www.tsa.gov. Have your passport, boarding pass, and ID at the ready; this speeds up the line for the rest of us who are waiting behind you.

Helpful in-flight tips. What to wear at 35,000 feet? Many airlines ensure the cabin temperature on long-haul flights is 'colder than a well-digger's bottom'. So please, avoid wearing shorts, T-shirts, and flip-flops for the trip. Why do you think they dole out blankets and socks in the amenity kits on board? I've noticed over the past few years, many in-the-know long-haul travelers tote along jogging outfits to don after take-off and just before bedding down.

Exercise aboard. I know the flight staff don't like it much, but I do get out of my seat and move about the cabin when the seatbelt sign is switched off. I try not to do this while the crew is serving meals or pushing the duty-free carts about the cabin. Every international airline has a website to make suggestions for staying in good gip at 35,000 feet. Try www.businesstravellogue.com.

I've learned the hard way if you want to arrive in good shape, tread lightly on alcohol intake. Drink plenty of water, and do some stretching and in-seat exercises during the flight. If you've got small children in tow, smile nicely at the cabin crew and ask if they have a child's kit. These kits have traditionally been free for the asking and include crayons and coloring books, puzzles, games, and the occasional deck of cards. When my troops were younger, and I didn't have time to stop for toys to bring home, I'd score a few of these to get me safely through our front door. With many airlines determined to add to in-flight revenue, some have started charging for these little ditties so ask first if they're on the house.

After touchdown tips. I've heard of perhaps a hundred different remedies and concoctions for 'jet-lag'. And I've tried maybe half of them. For a fellow who has flown around the planet about 28 times now, I've still not landed on one that really eliminates that 'drunken sailor' feeling I have for the first day on American soil. But I have also confirmed a few things that really make getting my body clock tick in time to the Yanks' over years of trial and error. I try to stay awake or go to sleep using the local time on the first night of arrival, even if it's a tough slog. I've learned not to drink alcohol on board, but more importantly for me, I drink gallons upon gallons of water and juice on the flight. Which is also why I insist on an aisle seat for frequent up and down travel to the toilets. When I'm on the ground, my

Touch-down in the USA—a few formalities and you're in!

temptation is to eat up big time, but I try to stick to salads and lighter fare for the first few days—which is hard going for a guy who likes the massive menus and platters full of food within my sights. And I read instead of flicking channels on the TV. I'm not sure if anyone has ever undertaken a study of what reading actually does to the body and the brain, but for me, it really works wonders. Stay clear of big drinking bouts on arrival as well, which can prolong the body's adapting to the new venue.

My favorite tail-feathers to fly. Naturally, I've got my airline A-list of favorite tail-feathers. These are usually connected to my love of frequent flyer miles and the accumulation of points. I love the notion that every time I fly, I'm also getting closer to a free ride, and if you are not a frequent flier member of the airline you're traveling to the USA on, sign up before you go. I'm partial to Hawaiian Airlines, anything Virgin, United and Qantas, Air Tahiti Nui, Delta Airlines and Air New Zealand for our long-haul flights to the USA. All have significant websites of their own and links to their other airline partners.

③. Bus, train, and local transport

As a general rule: 'When in Rome, do as the Romans do.' If you simply follow the local norm for how to get about in the USA, you'll get along just fine.

Leaving town. If your vacation plans take you out of the city limits and onto the open road to other parts of the 'real America', you'll need to hook-up the mode of transportation that best suits your plans and needs. If having the freedom to stop and go as you please is important to you, you'll need independent transportation. Buses, trams, motor coaches, trains, and other forms of mass transport don't make photo stops. For long-haul travel, in between cities or national parks venues, you'll

Look around—if the locals are using it, you should too

want to check on bus or rail services. In this next section, we've carved out a few of the major gateway cities for international arrivals into the USA so you can see how the locals do it just to get you started. Remember, because you've got an uncle in the business, feel free to ask us for specifics at www.overeasyguides. com.

Manhattan, New York Take the subway! When the doors open, jump on. The city moves at a caffeine rush 24 hours a day. New York City boasts over 8 million people living within its five boroughs, and that's comparatively tight quarters compared to other urban areas of the USA. To rent a car to get around Manhattan would be madness, so save any car hire for the day you're planning to leave the 'Big Apple' of New York. This is exactly what the locals do when they're lighting out for weekends, or getaway retreats to slopes, the 'Hamptons', or the nearby Catskill Mountains. If you do plan to leave Manhattan Island by car, aim to avoid Friday afternoons and any afternoon at rush hour which starts at about 4pm and goes on for hours. Also, during peak hours, New York's finest cops stand on street corners to write tickets for 'grid-lockers'—drivers who are caught in the middle of intersections when their lights turn red. Do NOT enter a NY intersection unless you've got a clear shot to get completely across. Even if you don't attract a ticket, you'll get plenty of guff from both pedestrians and other drivers. The same thing applies when you're on foot, cross at the crosswalks and avoid 'jay-walking' citations.

New York's subway, ferry, water taxi, bus, and rail system, and helicopter service are remarkable. Excellent, in fact. Get aboard the Staten Island Ferry and stay there for a few crossings. It has been free, but even if it costs a token, you'll enjoy the best Manhattan skyline vistas, the Statue of Liberty, the Hudson River

Leave the driving to the pros or take the bus in places like the Big Apple—you've got enough to look at.

and more, while enjoying a Coney Island hotdog and chatting up the locals. The Metropolitan Transportation System hosts its own museum, and for maps try www.mta.info.

Nail yourself a CityPass for New York if you want to do the museums, Empire State Building, and others. It will save you time and money. Try www.citypass.com. Walking in New York City is fantastic because the city is set up on a grid system. Streets, for the most part run from east to west, and avenues run from north to south.

My favourites while in New York include: the NY water taxis, a Slice of Brooklyn tours, Bike N Roll rentals, NY Helicopter Flight Services and booming big-time for overseas visitors, Brooklyn. Jump onto Brooklyn Tourism's website! This borough is blossoming all over. Nail yourself last minute tickets via StubHub—you'll be amazed at what they have going for good deals, and even 'not possible' tickets to shows and sporting events on the day!

Grab a free map from the hotel desk or the NYC & Company Visitor Information Center (www.nycvisit.com) on Broadway. If you've worn out the shoe leather in the Big Apple, just step to the curb and flag down (raise your arm into the air to resemble the lantern lady of the Statue of Liberty) or whistle for a yellow-metered cab. These yellow cabs are everywhere, weaving a tapestry of yellow through the traffic. Hold on tight. Cabs, shuttle buses, private cars, and limos line up outside of arrival terminals at all the major New York airports (JFK, LaGuardia, and Newark NJ). Legislation in place regarding cab fares now regulates how much you'll pay to get onto Manhattan Island. Check at the curb before loading up your luggage. For my money, I pre-book a black limo or 'town car' to collect me. It costs a bit more than a yellow cab, but I like the idea of my black-tie chauffeur waiting for me outside of baggage claim, and whisking me to my hotel (I love the Hotel Beacon!

Day or night—take a bite! The best is the Big Apple.

www.beaconhotel.com) like a hotshot. Then I avoid any lines with other folks going to 'my' city.

Boston, Massachusetts

Even the locals who live there get lost in Boston when driving. Public transport is the way to get about and ask for help: You'll fall in love with the New England accent. Talk sports in this town because the locals are fans-fantastic and fanatic. Boston was built on a traditional hub and 'square' or 'commons' network, which suggests that it's hard to find any logic in its layout for the outsider. Boston is a magnificent city for walking, and entire historic walks have been set aside, such as 'The Freedom Trail' (www.thefreedomtrail.org) which is a redbrick patch of pavement running 2.5 miles through the city and is a time machine for turning back the clock and bringing the history of the city to life. Our best advice is to hoof it or go with public transport: trams, trolleys, buses, and trains will get you to nearby Harvard Square, Fenway Park for the Red Sox games, and beyond. Sit in front of your morning cuppa and have a good plan in mind before heading out. If you want to cover the city by land and sea, sign up for Boston Duck Tours—they do a wonderful narration of the city sights and you travel in a World War II-type amphibious vehicle so they beat the traffic and go into the drink for short-cuts. Ask to drive! Try www.

'Beantown' Boston is best explored on foot—follow the freedom trail

bostonducktours.com. A Boston City map in the backpack or back pocket is essential. If you know where you want to get to, try www.hopstop.com, which gives directions for a number of American venues and cities in detail. If you do drive, keep in mind that New Englanders have a reputation for making turns without using their indicators. You've been warned.

Washington DC

Washington, the nation's capital, is like Boston. It's laid out on a central spoke system of roads. These inter-connected circles link to other hubs and spokes. So expect to get lost if you drive. The anchor landmarks of the Mall are the Capitol Building at one end and the Washington Monument at the other. Find a good place to park for the day. Then you're free to walk and enjoy and explore all Washington DC has to offer; most of it completely free of charge!

Motorized 'surreys' ply the mall area, and a single pass for step-on and step-off use is a bargain and saves significant shoe leather. These shuttles ply all the top spots, such as Arlington Cemetery, the tomb of the Unknown Soldier, the Kennedy gravesites, the FBI tour, the Capitol Building, Washington Monument, Jefferson Memorial, the White House, Lincoln Memorial, the Air and Space Museum, and an entire slew of Smithsonian Institute buildings, all of which are free for the taking. Try www.washington.org for details.

Bring your passport along as ID for some of the more secure venues. You don't have to stay in the 'District' if you've got wheels. Many folks cross the Potomac River and stay in places like Reston, or Falls Church, Virginia.

Like Boston, Washington DC has its own version of Duck tours on land and water, which are fun for kids and adults alike. Try www.dcducks.com or book it all as part of a package at www.

zuji.com and save by packaging up the costs for beds and sightseeing while you're in 'Beantown'.

Miami, Florida

Unless your holiday plans concentrate on beachfront activities, sun worshiping, long strolls along the sand, and staying put, you'll want a car to get around. Many of the places of interest in and around Miami, such as Coconut Grove and Coral Gables, are best accessed by a car, and day trips are not uncommon or hard to organize. Ethnic neighborhoods like 'Little Havana' are worth a visit and my all-time favorite is the 'cruise by car' along Ocean Blvd. at South Beach with the art deco architecture everywhere.

Car hire in Florida is cheap by comparison to other states, simply because there is a great deal of competition, so shop around. My all-time favorites remain constant because I can use my 'VIP Card' status with each to cut the lines, and accumulate those all-important frequent flier' points. ALAMO is my number one choice (www.alamo.com). Hertz, Enterprise, and Avis car rentals also have depots almost everywhere, and the variety of cars on offer varies widely. Kick the tires. Shop around on the net to get exactly what you want.

Orlando, Florida

Unless you're planning on staying inside the gates of Disney World and the Epcot Center (which many people do because it takes weeks to ride all the attractions) you'll want to rent a vehicle. Driving in Florida is easy, with plentiful road signage and very flat roadways that link up major points of interest and attractions. Florida, also known as 'the Sunshine State' attracts many Americans each year on vacation, and campgrounds and Recreational Vehicle Parks cater to this audience with on-site amenities such as waterslides and pools, games rooms, general stores, shops, golf, and more to lure your 'rig' in. Try www.visitflorida.com. Florida, for our money, is the best place to try out the RV scene for you. Roads are smooth, well signposted, and it is easy. Drive-away holidays in Florida can be very varied, from abundant amusement parks, to the Everglades, to the Gulf of Mexico, the Florida Keys, NASA Space Center, and the Atlantic beachfront. As with Miami, shop around for cars and if you want to try the ever-popular Recreational Vehicle Route, try our favorite, El Monte RV (www.elmonterv.com).

Orlando is also a great place to feel like a millionaire, renting your own mansion-style house. My favorite company for places to stay across the USA is 'A-1 Vacation rentals' at www.a1vacations.com with pool, mod cons for less than a hotel room and you get

Wear comfy shoes in DC. Walk everywhere.

to peek over the fence into how well-heeled Americans live.

In the West, major gateway cities vary on the best way of getting around.

San Francisco, California

The 'City by the Bay' is built on a significant number of hills that make it a prime candidate for mass transportation. The locals agree that getting around aboard its fabled cable cars or ferries is not only functional, but it's heaps of fun. The BART System (Bay Area Rapid Transit) of trains and buses is also extremely efficient and economical but for day touring, take to the streets and check in with www.onlyinsanfrancsico.com.

There are a few places you'd want to have wheels for, but you can hire a car for a day to do these. Muir Woods National Monument is an easy drive over the Golden Gate Bridge and up the coast. There you can walk among a stand of giant redwood trees, some of the oldest living things on planet earth and many on earth before the birth of Christ. Visit www.visitmuirwoods.com for the lowdown on the tall trees.

Other venues you might need for day tripping could include the Napa Valley, Sonoma, the Winchester Mystery House, Six Flags, and the gold rush ghost town restoration of Columbia. Otherwise, get out the comfy walking shoes and make your way to Fisherman's Wharf, Union Square shopping, the Museums, Alcatraz, and others. If you're going to a ball game in San Francisco, public transport will get you there. The State of California is massive, and the official website is well worth a pre-arrival visit. Go to www.visitcalifornia.com.

My home away from home in San Francisco is the Handlery Hotel on Union Square. Just one stay in this property and you're hooked, and the location is simply the best. Say hi to Jon Handlery while you're there—it's a very friendly family-run

Slow the pace and savor the place

property. Try www.handlery.com.

Los Angeles, California

'LA' was created and built for the car, when gasoline prices idled around 4 cents an imperial gallon. Plan to get behind the wheel in this sprawling 'suburb in search of a city' that is home to thousands of miles of multi-lane LA freeways and roads. Points of interest are spread far and wide in LA so jump onto www. lacity.org for some fast lane information about the area.

Because the city is home to 3.5 million or more Americans connected by roadways, major attractions are spread helter-skelter. To the north of LAX (the airport) is West Hollywood (www. visitwesthollywood.org), Rodeo Drive, Santa Monica, Universal Studios, the J. Paul Getty Museum, and others while to the south you've got Hermosa Beach, Anaheim, and Orange (www.

Rub elbows with the locals everywhere in America

anheimoc.org) County, boasting Disneyland and Knottsberry Farm to name only a few. There is a whole lot of LA in between these two areas to look at as well.

Rent a car and pre-plan your trips so you know which way you're headed out of the hotel. Our overall recommendation in LA is not to get behind the wheel on day one. Give yourself a day or two to get acclimatized to driving on the wrong side of the road (and looking the other way when stepping off the curb!)

I usually stay for a night or two on arrival at a hotel near the airport, where they provide free shuttle services to nearby shopping malls, car hire, and back to the airport. Once I've got my bearings, I catch the free shuttle to pick up my rental car. My favorite spot for getting settled in, especially when I'm with my family, is the Hacienda Hotel, (www.haciendahotel.com). The garden rooms are family-sized huge, the staff very family friendly, and costs won't break the budget. If I'm in town on business, it's the LAX Hilton Hotel (www.hiltonfamily.com) on Century Blvd. for the buffet and the executive floor attention I get. And if it's all out celebrity spotting and living rich, I'm all for the Beverly Hills Hotel and its celebrity status Polo Bar: Try www.westland.net for that rich and famous feeling—bring money.

Rental car outfits in LA offer GPS systems that can take you to and from places in a variety of languages, and you can even alter the gender if you prefer taking directions from a lad or a lass.

Public transport in LA is, in our view, pathetic but the locals are at least making a stab at it. Remember to drive on the right, the fast lane is to the extreme left, and if you're taking advantage of an 'express lane' you'd better have more than two people in tow. For all the myriad of roadways and freeways, expect traffic. Try www.aaccessmaps.com.

Las Vegas, Nevada

Go ahead—pre-book a 40-foot hummer or super-stretch limo to pick you up at the airport, and then, simply hoof it around Las Vegas after that. Las Vegas is easy, as it's smack-dab in the center of some pretty significant desert. For all intents and purposes, Las Vegas is basically built around two areas, the Las Vegas 'Strip' and the traditional gambling and entertainment mecca of downtown along Freemont Street.

Most visitors take to the streets only after dark when the lights dazzle and temperatures cool. My favorite place to stay in Vegas is the Planet Hollywood Resort and Casino (www. planethollywood.com) because of the shopping mall in-house, and the great eateries.

Pay-as-you-go trams and trolleys ply the major arteries, cabs are easy to catch from the hotel and casino foyers, and some resorts have now connected the dots between casinos with skyways and monorails so you never have to step out into the desert heat.

Out-of-town operators for Grand Canyon flight-seeing, adventure touring companies, and other attractions offer free pick-up and drop-off door to door for your dollar. If you're lighting-out from Las Vegas for Lake Mead, or the Grand Canyon, Bryce, or Zion Canyon National Parks, you'll want wheels.

Las Vegas is another place we'd recommend trying out an RV. El Monte RV (www.elmonterv.com) rentals has heaps of variety in the fleet and provides airport or hotel pick-ups and drop-offs on the house. There are other car hire and RV rental outfits around, so do your homework to get exactly what you want. Mind you, renting a Ferrari limits your luggage capacity and tends to be pricey, but you only go around once, and Las Vegas is a place where people go to break away from their everyday routine.

Try doing something different—you're on 'vacation'

Long-haul travel by bus and train

One of my earliest travel recollections was a Greyhound bus trip I took as a kid from Cleveland, Ohio to Orlando, Florida. Greyhounds' slogan then was 'Take the bus and leave the driving to us!' which sticks in my memory to this day. Getting around in America by bus in short bursts, and in-between places, is clean, safe, and comfortable. Bus routes often make stops in towns not normally serviced by rail, so if you're headed for that remote venue, a bus is a decent alternative to renting a vehicle and going it on your own. If you're using the bus between major cities and long-haul venues, hunt for an 'express' departure that reduces the number of 'milk run' stops in places you've never heard of, and will never likely re-visit.

Every major bus these days is equipped with mod cons, and all have toilets, reclining seats, overhead storage, reading lights, and other amenities. When considering the bus, check your

Take your lead on getting around from the locals

'ETA' (estimated time of arrival) with the bus line. As buses ply the super-slabs and back roads on a 24-hour, 7-day basis, you could rock up at your destination at 3:36am on a Tuesday night when the town is locked up tight, local cabbies have gone home to bed, and the neon 'no vacancy' sign is illuminated in the only hotel across the road. Also when the buses do make stops to switch over drivers (a bit like the old Pony Express when they swapped mounts and riders at intervals), you're compelled to get off the bus and stretch your legs in some locations that are less than attractive.

Mind you, there are millions of folks who swear by the bus as a great magic carpet to get you around, and you can pre-purchase bus passes with some outfits that offer unlimited travel for a specified period. Check with the American Bus Association (ABA) on www.buses.org or Greyhound on www.greyhound.com.

However, for my money, I'd still rather take the train.

Taking the train

For a few dollars more, I prefer train travel over the bus when going 'point to point' in the USA. First up, I like to move about and on the train I've got a lot more carriage to carry on in. Also, the seats are generally larger, with a deeper gradient of recline in coach class and if I really want to splurge, I can get a first-class cabin, with a full on drop-down bed where I get myself lulled to sleep with the clickity-clack motion of the rails.

Train travel can be another way to have your bed and get there too. Many students or budget-strapped visitors use night trains in between cities as a way to get there and bed-down in the same stroke. Just remember to bring your own pillow.

Being a 'talker', I appreciate the fact that on board the train, I can engage the staff, porters, café and dining car staff, and other passengers are easily accessible. I have more mobility to pick up and set down as I please en route, something I could never get away with when traveling by bus because you're not meant to engage the driver at all while underway for obvious safety considerations.

Some American trains are special, and some routes cater to overseas guests with gusto. Train travel between major coastal cities on the East Coast and West Coast cover some majestic and scenic routes and the first class cabins are well-worth the investment. Some even offer sky-dome and scenic viewing carriages. Check www.railplus.com and www.amtrak.com for more details.

4. Organized and escorted tours

One of the things I love about fully escorted touring is that I can simply sit back, relax, and take it all in. I've got someone at the front of the coach to look after the driving, the parking,

You meet some of the nicest folks on tour

the historical narration, and attending to the admissions details at check-in. And because these companies buy in bulk, I love cutting the lines at attractions. These escorted tours also allow me more time to chat up the other like-minded travelers and enjoy the sites and scenery without fretting about the next night stop, city navigation, or speed trap. For many people, escorted tour packages also represent excellent value because you're buying your beds, entries, meals, transportation, portage, tips, and other items in bulk via the tour operator, often at significant savings.

Among those-in-the-know who travel on fully escorted motor-coach holidays, there is a way of dissecting the 'colored pencils' copy in the glossy pages to identify the value for money element of what you get for your money. It's called the 'See, View, or Visit' test.

When the brochures' pages lure would-be travelers, they might not be totally upfront on how they present what's included' in the cost of the basic holiday. One of the reasons for this is that many firms pay the tour directors an on-board pittance per day, but reward them financially with fat commissions on selling the optional tours and excursions, evening meals out and other add-ons, which can, in some cases, almost double the costs of the original tour package.

Our reason for bringing this fact to light is not to condone or condemn this long-standing marketing tool by the tour operators, but to suggest the addition to the list of another key word, 'experience'.

Shop around because many operators offer special itineraries, with a huge variety of duration, night stops, age, group size, and pace to match almost any interest and budget. The best advice we can give when exploring these escorted options is to do your homework before booking anything and compare what you get.

Tours come in all shapes and sizes—select carefully

Tour operators are well known for inferring or implying the attractions and inclusions for each itinerary, so be aware. Words such as 'See', 'View', and 'Visit' take on entirely new meanings when selecting an escorted coach holiday, so ask about 'Options' while on tour. These are items you'll be paying extra for, as they are not included in the basic cost of the package. Another thing to keep in mind, is that the tour director and drivers expect a tip or gratuity at the end of your holiday—standard operating practice that can work out to be a dollar a day for both the driver and escort, usually slipped to the team on the last day or at a bon voyage and farewell gathering.

Visit your local travel agent, who'll give you a number of brochures but don't settle there. Other agents will have their preferred operators, often based on better commission levels they can earn.

My all time favorites for young travelers are, TrekAmerica www.trekamerica.com and All-Star Adventures www.allstartrips.

Speciality travel is booming—take a tour that fits you to a 'T'

com. For fully escorted motor-coach tours, I'm partial to APT www.apttouring.com.au, Tauck Tours www.tauck.com, Insight Vacations www.insightvacations.com, and ATI www.americantours.com, which provides coach tours for hundreds of travel companies worldwide. Last but in no way least, Footloose Tours are for small groups and open-age travel www.footloose.com.

If your holiday plans include making a difference, or getting some worthwhile dirt under your fingernails, look into joining an International Field Research Expedition with EARTHWATCH www.earthwatch.org. This non-profit organization lets you make a difference, while enjoying the company and camaraderie of other like-minded folks to actually 'get stuck into' a real field research effort.

Other outfits also offer experiential travel options that scratch below the surface and cater to special interests in America. The National Geographic Society and the NY Museum of Natural History also offer similar programs.

I've discovered the very best source for tracking these non-mainstream opportunities is the travel trade's bible known as the Specialty Travel Index that covers everything from chocolate tours to white-water rafting, to religious pilgrimages, to floral festivals, and beyond. Go to www.specialtytravel.com. Go ahead and subscribe; it is great armchair reading even if you never leave the house.

5. Hiring cars, motorhomes, and motorbikes

With millions of miles of paved roads, it will come as no surprise that almost any kind of vehicle can be hired for a price in the States. From Ferraris, to Harley Davidsons, to hummers and all-terrain vehicles, from luxury motorhomes to mopeds, in-line skates, and electric golf carts. If it's got wheels, the Americans will rent it to you. In almost every case, you'll need a valid license and credit card (even for renting a bike or blades, you'll need to show proof of identity). Most rental car, RV, and motorcycle firms have age restrictions for drivers under the age of 25, but shop around and be prepared to pay more.

In past years, younger drivers who had more time on their hands could easily buy a vehicle, use it for their trip and sell it at journey's end. This practice is becoming increasing difficult with state requirements for insurance and a permanent address. It should go without saying that you should do a 'once-over' of any hire vehicle before driving it off the lot. You'll want to confirm in writing any pre-existing damage or scratches, dings, bings, or bumps beforehand, so you're not charged for any damages caused by the person before you.

I've become a walking advertisement for renting a Recreational Vehicle in the USA. These motorhomes are a cinch to drive, have all the creature comforts, and I only unpack my bags once. Add to this the fact that I've got my transportation and my beds for the same buck, and I'm double pleased. But the real magnet for RVing around America is the opportunity it affords to mix it up with the Americans themselves who spend millions of bed nights each year in camping and RV grounds across the country. RV resorts, campground, and national parks camping areas are wonderful. Many have full hook-ups, pools, general stores, and more, and if they are bare-bones venues, it is for good reason: the natural surroundings speak for themselves. Travel by RV gives new meaning to the freedom of the open road and independent travel. I'm wholly hooked on the guys of El Monte because they have motorhome depots all over the place, and most importantly for me, they

Don't pass up a chance to try Cadillac camping

rent to a significant American audience so there are not massive billboard advertisements for the company plastered all over the RV which scream 'Tourist' to every Tom, Dick, and Henrietta who overtakes us on the turns. Book up with www.elmonterv.com.

When I rent a car, I book the vehicle that best suits my travel plans. If I've got the kids in tow, we tackle the people-movers because the kids can stretch out, and we're not sardined-in for the luggage space. If I'm 'on call' and will be having clients aboard, I'll go with the big luxury wheels, plush leather interiors, and sound systems like a big Cadillac or Lincoln. And when I'm on my own, doing heaps of parking up and pulling out again stops, I go for a small, compact car that runs on near-fumes and is easy to maneuver in and out of the tight spots. When selecting a type of car you'll need, take all the factors into account before booking.

Roughing it American style—all the creature comforts laid on

Be sure you've signed up in advance for the rental car's priority club, so you can go to the head of the class and cut through the lines for the red carpet treatment. It doesn't cost anything to sign up in most cases and even if you only use the priority status once, you're ahead of the game. I also make certain I can accumulate frequent flier points for any care hire I'm doing. My best buy for automobiles is Alamo at www.alamo.com.

There are a few national outfits who rent motorcycles, ski-doos, and all-terrain vehicles from under one roof. Restrictions do apply, and in many cases you'll need to undergo an 'orientation' to assure the rental company you know what you're doing before you drive off the lot. My pick of the litter for handsome Harley Davidson hiring is Eagle Rider Rentals because they have switched-on staff, and depots in all the right places for starting off or ending up. Try www.eaglerider.com.

⑥. Travelers: women, disabled, seniors, and families with children

Across the board, travel in the USA appears easier for families, folks with disabilities, seniors, and women than many other international destinations. Handicapped or 'impaired' travelers to the USA will soon discover that the Americans have done a great deal of 'mainstreaming' and providing easier access to the handicapped or challenged traveler.

In fact, legislation has been in place for years, mandating the provision of access to public buildings, national parks, and attractions for challenged travelers. Laws governing any new construction require that this audience is taken into full consideration.

Specially designated parking places, camping sites, restroom facilities, lifts, ramps, and other amenities make getting around, for the most part easy navigations. Special attention has also

The USA has something for everyone.

be given to the hearing and visually impaired in America. One place to look is www.usatourist.com. Another non-profit group is Mobility International. If you have a home-country 'disabled tag' for parking, bring it along in the (www.miusa.org) luggage. The Specialty Travel Index is published in magazine format twice each year, and lists over 150 tour companies, retailers, and expedition planners who cater to travel with special needs. Subscribe to the magazine or jump onto the site for a birds' eye view at www.specialtytravel.com.

Travel with children in America is not a chore. Almost everywhere, families with kids are welcomed, and in many cases, given fast-track entry, eats, or beverages for free. Americans go everywhere with the kids, so you're expected and welcomed well throughout the USA. If they don't want the kids along, they'll send out the message loud and clear long before you ever get to the front door, as some 'adults-only' resorts, singles spas, and

Air, water or land, you'll find what you like in the USA

Women travel in the USA easily

retreats make no bones about leaving the kids at home.

My all-time favorite publications for tracking travel with teens and tots are Out & About with Kids www.outandaboutwith kids. com.au and Holidays with Kids www.holidayswithkids.com.au. If I'm seeking before-I-go advice on travel with the troops in tow, I speak to a travel agent who has 'been there and done it' with the kids.

First-hand knowledge when going places with families is worth its weight in gold when it comes to eliminating the potential for disasters. When we had our first trip with our first child, my young and single and childless travel agent booked us into a hotel in central London, which was so small you could not swing a cat, never mind a child, around. The agent 'hadn't even thought about that' when making the booking, as in previous years it had only been myself and my wife going along. To compound this oversight, we were on the 8th floor with no secure lock on the balcony door or windows, kids paid full tariff at the breakfast table, no room service or kids menu was available, and there was a hefty additional cost for a roll-away cot which we didn't have room for in our splinter-sized room anyhow. The most important consideration to take on board when traveling with your offspring is to simply slow down the pace. Avoid single-night stops, pack-ups, and take-offs. Trust me, you'll need the extra time and with a few days in each venue, your kids will connect with other kids. Everyone wins. Another venue on the net with good ideas for moving around America with the troops in tow is www. familytravelnetwork.com.

When we travel with the kids we create significant laundry. So we simply carry along a soft-sided duffle bag and pack it on the top of the suitcases with the detergent. If we stop for lunch en route, we can oftentimes pop the laundry in, stroll the main streets of Tombstone Arizona, pop into the OK Corral, have a 'sasparila', and conquer the colors and whites in the same stroke. Laundramats are abundant in the States, and many campgrounds, RV parks, hotels, and inns have on-site facilities. Beware: If you hand your dirty items over to the hotel in those nice bags they provide, it'll cost you a bomb. Feel free to share your own musings on travel with the kids, and your own take on where the missing socks wind up on www.overeasyguides.com.

For women traveling in America, the country poses no real hardship, compared with some of the challenges for female travelers and solo sojourns in undeveloped countries. For the inside word, helpful hints, and happenings for women on the move, try www.womentraveltips.com. Although a number of the helpful hints and tips apply to travel outside the USA, a great deal of the sound advice can be applied to independent travel anywhere, including America. A quick peek at the listings for women's travel options in the Specialty Travel Index reveals

Go ahead, take the plunge—America is awesome at any age

over 100 outfits that cater to single women worldwide. Try www.specialtyteavel.com. Hundreds of BLOG sites have also been created with some offering helpful hints, places that cater to, and places to stay clear of, straight from the female perspective.

For seniors, the US government has dedicated hundreds of pages, links, articles, and other items of interest to this significant portion of the traveling public. On the website for the USA, there are specific areas for visiting seniors. Try www.usa.gov and search in the 'Seniors' and 'Seniors Travel' sections. Another group that offers information to its members is the AARP (American Association of Retired Persons) at www.aarp.org. Membership brings a number of benefits, including some seductive discounts. Overseas seniors who visit the USA should pack along similar membership credentials as the discounts are often honored as well. Simply showing a seniors card from your home country is often sufficient to get you to the front of the line, attract the discounts, and speed you on your way.

7. Food and drink

I was amazed by the friendliness of our waitress, but it took us a good 20 minutes to order. Once we'd been walked through the 24-hour breakfast menu, we took the easy route and order the # 3 special... and then it all started. There was the offer of our eggs, with a dozen variations, then the toast, and finally milk varieties, juices, the bottomless cup of coffee. My partner jokingly suggested we'd need a nap after our meal just to recuperate, and that throwaway comment was made before we saw the SIZE of the portions—no wonder Americans came up with the idea of a 'doggie bag'!

Don't expect to lose weight when visiting the USA. Because of the larger than expected portions and eating habits of the Americans, you need to prepare yourself for gaining a few kilos while you're visiting. If you're careful, however, you should be burning up more energy on holiday and keeping your waistline in order.

The Americans introduced the bottomless cup and unlimited refills, and loading up any drink container to the brim with ice. And they also introduced the 'doggie bag' for a very good reason: You couldn't possibly eat everything in one sitting. Americans love their cold drinks very cold. So be prepared to manhandle a massive, more-than-a-handful container. Over the past 25 years, 'the more is better' and 'super-sizing' competitive nature of food vendors and the value-added business community have created their own monsters. Plentiful proportions are today the reason for concern among health officials about the growing size of Americans. It's hard to stay trim when an entire nation is accustomed to digesting a platter of good food that is half the size of the state of Rhode Island. Americans make no bones

Don't expect to lose weight in America

Plentiful portions—ask for a 'doggie bag'!

about being BIG; as travelers, just try not to get caught up in all those readily-available calories. Our general rule when selecting dining options is simple: fast-food is 'some-time food' and we pick wisely when we do exercise this eating option.

Actually, the availability of wholesome, fresh food is never very far away. Supermarkets, organic, and community co-ops abound. Even if your travel plans don't include self-catering, Americans' boast city parks, many with barbeque grills, community centers, and other places where you can whip up your own culinary delights 'on the house'. Simply shop for yourself at the local supermarket and make a picnic or barbeque in a quiet lovely setting.

If you're on the move in a car or RV then an inexpensive 'esky' cooler/ice chest bought from the local supermarket will preserve food and keep drinks cold and they fit easily inside the cabin, between the seats, or in the 'trunk.'

Drinking In America. In 1984 new legislation made the minimum drinking in the USA the highest in the world. Prior to 1984, the drinking age in the USA was almost a potluck situation, with each state pinning a legal age that suited. Some states also allowed the drinking of low-octane 'hooch' or 3.2% beer at the ripe old age of 17, while a neighboring state insisted that its drinkers be 18 years old, and another neighbor-state pegged the legal drinking age at 21 years of age. Naturally this situation led to underage drinkers in one state simply popping over the state line to catch themselves a legal buzz in another.

This art of border hopping for 'hooch' liquor led to a massive road-kill statistic, from which there appeared to be no resolution. In 1984, legislators and voters, tired of burying their young, came up with a plan that lifted the legal drinking age in all 50 states to 21 years of age, the highest in the modern world. The National Minimum Drinking Age Act of 1984 required all states to raise

Ask the locals about the best eats

their purchase and public possession of alcohol age to 21, or risk losing federal highway funds under the Federal Highway Aid Act (and just to keep the record straight, we're talking billions of dollars here). So it is no surprise that by 1987, all states had complied with the 21 minimum age law.

Have your ID ready for the check-out clerk in the supermarket or liquor store. They seem to ask everybody for ID, as they are required to by law. For exceptions to this legislation, try www2.potsdam.ed. In many states, the levels for drink-driving are slightly higher than ours, with alcohol blood levels for intoxication set at .08. You need to check on this as plans are in motion to make changes. The best rule is simply 'Don't drink and drive'. If you are going to sample the local brew, determine a designated driver in advance as vehicle hire firms have disclaimers and waivers in place if you have a collision or get locked up for over imbibing.

Ⓧ. Sleeping around in America
—Accommodation

'Sleeping around' in America is easy. Major hotel and motor inn chains, B&Bs, campground organizations, dude ranches, university dormitories and national parks are only a few of the mainstream choices for places to stay in the USA.

Hotels, resorts and the big hotel chains

I've changed the way I book my beds in the USA. I once selected my property based on price and location alone. These days with my frequent flier memberships and preferred status cards, I stick to the places that I know will provide me with a good bed at mates' rates and I can circumvent the long lines and do a priority check-in.

For me, it's no longer about the money but it's about the time

Something on the American menu for everyone

I save getting in and out of beds. For this reason I love my Hilton buddies and the properties of the Starwood group of hotels. I use the internet big time to track down the best price, often linked to a domestic airfare, sightseeing pass, a transfer, or some other ingredient to add value and get a better deal for myself. Try www.travelocity.com or www.zuji.com. For specific properties look into www.hilton.com or www.starwoodhotels.com. These bigger accommodation 'brands' have multiple levels of properties on hand that can cater to a wide audience and you're sure to find something that fits the budget. Remember to ask for specials and packages no matter which property you select. Some bigger hotel groups have 'priority club' or 'executive floors' which are available at no extra cost, offer afternoon lounge drinks and nibbles, or a complimentary cup of coffee and croissant in the morning. Smaller, non-chain related properties can also provide a family-friendly approach to providing beds, and you'll soon have your own favorites.

Don't overlook those wonderful experiential places to bunk down either: the Dude Ranchers Association offers up over 100 ranch stay options in the USA for something different. Try www.duderanch.org. Dude Ranches are not just accommodation options. A dude ranch stay IS the destination, linked to activities like horse-riding, cattle drives, roping and rodeo events, wilderness rides, and other equestrian endeavors. Packages are almost always fully inclusive so you'll not be reaching into your wallet for options, extras, and meals as they're included in the overall package. Beds can vary from free-standing bunk houses to covered wagons and decadent tents depending on the ranch, so shop around for the one that makes you most comfortable in the saddle.

I'm going to take a few liberties here to highlight some of the hotels that have become my own 'home away from home'.

Bedding down is brilliant—pick whatever suits you

When I'm in San Francisco or San Diego, I sleep in Jon Handlery's hotels. This is the only hotel I've come across where each staff member treats the place as though they were the boss or had ownership in its success. Hotels have been in Jon's family for close to a hundred years. Go to www.handleryhotels.com.

In New York, it is either the Hotel Beacon (www.beaconhotel.com) or the Doubletree All-suites by Hilton (www.hiltonfamily.com) on Time Square.

My pick for Los Angeles continues to be the Hacienda Hotel LAX (www.haciendahotel.com) simply because of the helpful, friendly staff. This is a privately owned property near the airport with all the mod cons, and having staff greet me by name goes a long way when I'm staying in town for two to three weeks on end. The chicken soup in the restaurant is to die for and the prices are very reasonable.

In Hawaii, it's always been Starwood Hotels' 'Pink Palace'— The Royal Hawaiian because I like the idea of sleeping in palaces, and where royalty has previously bedded-down (www.starwoodhawaii.com). It's great for the service, and the name-dropping, but this hotel is under renovations, so check first. My other long-standing favorite in Hawaii is the Hilton (ww.w.hilton.com), as my troops love being smack-dab in the center of things for a few days, and then we rent a car and head for our own rented villa or estate from Hawaii Beach Homes at www.hawaii-beachhomes.com.

A word about being 'bumped'. Being 'bumped' is a fancy way of the hotel staff moving you to another property because theirs is currently 'over-booked'. If you have a confirmed reservation, take the 'bump' provided because it should be an upgrade of some sort for your inconvenience. Often the alternative is better than your original venue, or the offending property will toss in the buffet breakfast or a few cocktails or a room upgrade with a better view. Don't be offensive at the front desk. Simply ask for a modest compensation for your time and inconvenience.

Numerous American colleges and universities open their dorms and campuses to non-student guests, particularly during summer months when fully matriculated students are gone. Check these by specific area and venue, depending on your travel plans. The American Youth Hostels groups and YMCA hostels offer a wide variety of bed-down options. Some require you to be a member, which is generally not over the top cost-wise, and venues, locations, and facilities can vary widely, so check around before confirming your place. Try www.hiusa.com.

Camping in America is cushy. And you'll never suffer for choice or variety. Many of the 12,000 listed campgrounds with Camping USA at www.camping-usa.com run the spectrum of

Cadillac camping or all the creature comforts are available in America. Pick what pleases!

clothing optional (nudist camping?), pet-friendly (bring your own horse along), to beachfront, mountain top, and everything in between. Facilities vary from primitive and pristine, to downright decadent and luxurious and everything imaginable in between. As an alternative to staying in hotels or motor inns, even if you're not toting a tent along, look at camping grounds for their cabins or pre-erected canvas options. KOA, a group of franchised camping areas across America oftentimes offer 'KOA Kabins or Kottages' and the only thing you need to take is a sleeping bag. Try www.koa.com.

If you're going this route, sign up for a membership card as you'll be entitled to discounts and accumulation of rewards points. Ruby's Inn Campground outside of Bryce National Park offers up full RV hook-ups, tent sites, hotel rooms, family rooms, bunk houses, and a baker's dozen of traditional Native American tee-pees as alternatives to pitching your own tent. It is huge fun, and the novelty comes complete with all the bragging rights. Try www.rubysinn.com. Even Mickey Mouse has moved into the alternative accommodation act, with a range of permanent mobile homes on the Fort Wilderness portion of Disneyworld in Florida. Try www.disneyworld.disney.go.com. Staying in camping grounds and RV parks in the USA is simply the best way to really become ingrained and engage the Americans. Most of the Americans you camp alongside are on vacation, and often love making new friends with folks from overseas. For our money, camping in America is tops no matter how you do it: motorhome hire, a tent, tee-pees or pre-erected 'hard-top' options. Please, let us know how you went on www.overeasyguides.com because we love the feedback.

⑨. Entertainment and spectator sports

Ticket and event brokers across America seem to be able to come across with tickets, even when the odds seem against it happening. Travel websites or travel agents are also a source for connecting you to tickets.

Buying tickets through your favorite travel website or local agent has its advantages in that you can sometimes get a better deal than if you buy component parts from other supplier's piece-meal fashion. The other advantage is that if something goes awry in the bookings, or while you're on holiday, you've got someone or someplace to turn to where you're a valued client or customer. Online sites that do nothing but find tickets for USA events are also secure and well respected among the travel community. Try www.worldticketsales.com or www.frontrowusa.com. My pick for tickets has got to be StubHub, because the site has never failed to deliver me a ticket or two—even at the last minute www.stubhub.com.

In New York City, where everyone wants a 'bargain', you need to physically go to the 'Island' in the Center of Broadway and 47th Street to get half-price tickets for that day's performances. The significant sign over the kiosk reads 'TKTS', and the line can be long, but it moves quickly and while on the line, you'll be offered all manner of other entertainment options like buskers and free tickets to see live TV program filming, such as the David Letterman Show. Available tickets are on a first-come-first-served basis, so get to the TKTS kiosk early if you want tickets for a top Broadway production.

Promotional firms often use this line to hand over everything from free sunglasses to cosmetic samples so tote a shopping bag along to collect the goodies while you wait. If your must-see show is just not showing up on the cards, or you don't want

Speak sports and you're in

Your accent entitles you to celebrity status in the States

to risk a 'maybe seat', try Broadway and Theatre Direct on www. broadway.com. You'll pay a premium but you'll get what you want for doing so.

For Hollywood TV shows, or to be part of an audience, try for free tickets at www.hollywoodtickets.com. If you have a bit of time on your hands and want to be actively in a movie as an 'extra', there are websites and companies hired by the studios to locate crowds for major motion pictures. You'll be fed, but not paid and you'll have the bragging rights of saying you 'were in the picture' ... even if spotting you might require binoculars. Try www.bigcrowds.com for starters. You'll have to sign a waiver, saying you are happy to be in the flicks, but get yourselves a copy—they're suitable for framing!

West Hollywood, Memphis, Chicago blues, Louisiana jazz, Bourbon Street 'jams', western rodeos, film festivals, state fairs, and all major and minor league sports events offer general admission seating or 'standing room only'. It is only a matter of doing your homework in advance of your trip, and nailing down the tickets you want. Again, the web is a great way to help you find the tickets. Jump in with all fingers firing.

By the way, not all sporting event tickets will cost you money. Many B grade teams in baseball and 'winter camp' squads play to the crowd for free. And college sports events are significant in the America, with record-breaking crowds to some so again, check-in with the locals for what's up in your area.

For the major sporting venues and events like NFL football, baseball, golf, extreme sports, hockey, NASCAR racing, tennis and almost any other sporting event, try www.stubhub.com.

10 . Outdoor activities

If it's outdoor activities you've got on your agenda, you'll be very pleasantly surprised when reviewing the possibilities in the USA. *The Specialty Travel Index* (STI), a publication that has been exclusively used by travel agents worldwide is a great resource for digging deep in the area of outdoor activities. Get yourself a subscription at www.specialtytravel.com.

They provide short and sweet 'vignettes' of operators who do the entire 'ball and wax' of travel outside, such as bike riding, boogie boarding, cable car, canoeing, chuck wagon dinners, snorkeling, skiing, snowboarding, fishing, scenic flights, Disneyland, dune buggy, airboat rides, ghost towns, gold panning, grand canyon flights, horse riding, hot springs, hummer tour, Indian ruins and museums, jet boat ride, jet skiing, cavern tours, casino shows, limo rides, lobster bake, steamboat ride, native guided tours, Navajo Jeep Tours, para-sailing, rodeo, roller lading, roller coaster, sailing, San Diego Zoo, scuba diving, sea kayaking, Sea World, skateboarding, snow shoeing, sunset

Wear comfy shoes

sailboat cruise, swamp tour, Universal Studios, volcano hike, waverunners, Wet n Wild Parks, whaling museums, whitewater rafting, windsurfing, and wine tasting. And we haven't even got started!

The editors at STI pigeonhole each activity by 'region' and cross-reference by state as well, which makes fitting in activities you're hunting for with places you're most likely to locate them on offer. Try www.specialtytravel.com.

When in America, go for it! Try something you'd never do at home.

OUR "BEST OF THE BEST"
ACROSS
AMERICA

Making a list of favorites is a challenge because on every occasion my view is altered or impacted by the people I'd shared them alongside. We welcome feedback from this portion of the book, so feel free to bounce back with your top spots to www.overeasyguides.com. So, here's a pot-luck list of our best licks in the USA. Please let us hear from you for yours!

1. Best beaches

There is a great deal of coastal America, with some significant sand and surf to enjoy, almost all of it accessible to the general public. The US government has laid down exact data on the costal coverage and bodies of water for anyone willing to dive into the data on www.nationalatlas.gov. Please don't discount the lakes, rivers, and streams inland that may not be saltwater, surf, and sand dunes, but are just as attractive at any season.

A few bits of cultural protocol that seem to be unique in America come to mind. Although Americans are outgoing in nature, they cover up their 'privates' on the beaches. Nude bathers are subject to being arrested or fined, and even the act of going topless on most American beaches will raise more than eyebrows. Nude beaches can be found by shopping on the internet, and are usually connected to nudist colonies or retreat spas. Locals will tell you where the best 'unofficial' buff sites are located, so just ask around if you intend to shed more than your inhibitions. Many of the clothing optional beaches and venues in the USA are in private hands (pardon the pun) but peek over the fence at www.about.com, which has compiled a list of places by US states for consideration when going naked. Nailing down the beaches that best suit (or clothing optional) you is easy, if you again ask the locals. Go to www.americasbestonline.net for a full rundown on family beaches, nude venues, beaches

Handpick your place at the beach

with boardwalks, people-watching possibilities, and singles and surfing places as the best, according to the Americans themselves.

Also prepare yourself; in the land of the free and the home of the 'super-size' you might just catch sight of some significantly large Americans in the sun for fun. I think the terms like big, bold, and beautiful come to mind when some of America's population take to the shoreline. We only mention this so you might caution the children not to point or make size observations.

Here goes with my list, and remember hats, lotion, sunglasses, towels, and your accent are all required for a good day at the shoreline.

Panamá City, Florida. This beach, on the Gulf of Mexico and well-known as 'party-central', is big on clubs and pubs

Butt-naked or bring the entire brood—there's a beach with your name on it

along the dunes so practice your co-ed volleyball on the beach.

Black's Beach, La Jolla, CA. Used to be a butt-naked venue but town fathers put a lid on it in the late '70s. People still cheat, so look out for the hand-painted 'clothing optional' signs. Young, athletic crowd, attracts night owls.

Hampton's, Long Island NY. This stretch of beach and dunes is Manhattan's summer camp. Expect to dress for a night out, and meet with Manhattan's money during the day. Celebs mix it up with stockbrokers, traders, and social climbers, all on the same Dune Road stretch of multi-million dollar real estate. This is an articulate, well-heeled crowd, and summering in the Hamptons never goes out of fashion. I've met James Jones, Irwin Shaw, Truman Capote, Norman Mailer, Tennessee Williams, and others. Everyone walks the beach; there are miles of it, few public restrooms are in sight because the locals retreat up their private boardwalks to the mansion. Jim Flynn's www.bestweekends.com venue does a great job of this area.

Jones, Beach, Long Island New York. Just 33 miles from the Big Apple, this shares the exact dunes and sand as the Hamptons. It is not as far as the Hamptons or as exclusive. The rest of the Manhattan-ites and Long Islanders use this beachfront playground. It is open to the public, has miles of amenities and beach-goers can pick from a baker's dozen venues. Our pick is West End II because it's the home of a fair few well-heeled communities like Manhasset, Great Neck, and Sands Point. Lifeguards are on duty, they also have calm water beaches and two pools, food and beverages are available and you can hire bikes, play putt-putt golf and more at Jones Beach. Try www.nysparks.state.ny.

Catalina Island, California is just a boat ride from Los Angeles. This was once the private estate of the Wrigley gum family fortune with great, uncrowded beaches. Getting there is half the fun. You can camp or stay in a B&B overnight if you like. Bike, hike, or hire golf carts to get you around as there are very few cars on the Island. Try www.catalina.com as you'll need to get there by boat or plane—too far to swim it.

Tybee Island, Georgia. This is one of America's most laid-back beaches with beach bungalows and no two matching cottages for rent. They are very pet and family friendly in these parts. Beach-combing flotsam and jetsam have contributed to a lot of the local construction. Try www.mybeachhouseontybee. com.

Fort Lauderdale, Florida. Young and happening, this crowd spends days on the beach, nights in the clubs, and 'cruises' along Las Ollas Blvd. It's jammed with college kids during Easter Break and Spring breaks. Try www.sunny.org.

Venice Beach, CA. Home to the 'ocean front walk', although most beachgoers do it on skates and beach bikes these days. This is where you'll find hawkers, bars and cafes, muscle beach types, and plenty of people-watchers. Dive into www.beachcalifornia.com.

Cape May, New Jersey has a traditional 1930s feel to it, complete with wooden boardwalks, arcade games, and roller coaster rides along the Atlantic. It is not nearly as 'trendy' or showy' as the Hamptons. It has plenty of beautiful beachfront with all the allure of the Coney Island era. You can rent a cottage or beach bungalow here if you want to escape from the big cities and just chill. Try www.nj.com.

Santa Monica Fishing Pier, LA California. Hotdogs and corn-dawgs, arcade games, local fishing friends, and Ferris wheel are all happening on the pier. Underneath is the fiefdom of surfers, bikers, sunbathers, beach bunnies, and in-line skaters rule this surf and turf. Try www.santamonica.com.

Key West, Florida and the Florida Keys. Being only 90

Celebrate the differences on Catalina Island—that is a film star next to you!

Carnival coastline and 'cotton candy' parkside attractions

miles from Cuba, sunsets at Mallory's Wharf are a nightly ritual to watch the sun drop into the ocean, and signal another night of nocturnal revelry. This is party-town central with entertainments at Ernest Hemmingway and Tennessee Williams old watering holes. Try www.fla-keys.com.

Cape Cod, MA. The beaches 'of the cape' are most famous for the summer frolicking of the Kennedy family and the wild and wacky community of Provincetown on the Cape's tip-end. There's a beach for everyone, somewhere. Cape Cod can be cold in winter so don't even bother unless long walks in thermal gear is on your must-do-agenda. Try www.capeguide. com.

For all the beaches mentioned above, there will be heaps of information from the state websites. Remember to wear a hat, apply sunscreen, and engage the local beachcombers when visiting.

2. Best camping spots

Camping in the USA is of an extremely high standard, with many private and public camping grounds boasting hair dryers, saunas and spas, free movies, nightly entertainment, swimming pools, full 'RV hook-ups', and much more. Some of my favorites fall into the 'primitive' category, at the other end of the 'creature comforts scale' as they blend in well with the landscape, wildlife, and surroundings. The choices for camping and RVing are almost endless and you can choose to go bush or go *bourgeois*, or my favorite, a balanced mix of both.

There are a number of national chains and organizations dedicated to promoting camping across the country. One is called 'Camping USA' and they offer online assistance, and the 'heads-up' of the best places and discounts for camping. Try www.camphalfprice.com.

If you're strapped for cash, and need a place to park your Recreational Vehicle overnight, Wal-Mart and Sam's Club discount stores allow free overnight RV camping in the parking lot; just clear it with the store manager in advance. Go to the company's website, where they have a 'store-finder' dropdown, for finding your nearest venue. Try www.walmart.com.

Camping fees in the USA can run from free to as much as $40 per night depending on the location and facilities. It is a good idea to ask first, and shop around before selecting a place. Numerous franchise-type organizations offer camping facilities, such as KOK (Kampgrounds of America) at www.koa.com and Yogi Bear's Jellystone Parks at www.campjellystone.com.

Remember that Americans fill up campsites during the summer months, and many of the best places are on a 'first come, first served' basis. For many national parks, pre-booking

Bear Country

Black Bears may visit this area in search of food.
This could create problems for people and bears.
Please help us avoid this problem by:

* Storing all food in your vehicle
  or hard-sided RV, not in tents.
* Storing garbage in your vehicle
  and taking it home when you leave.

**Please don't contribute to
the delinquency of bears!**

The locals can be very, very, very friendly

is essential. Try the Department of the Interior for details of their 'park pass' and pre-booking sites: www.doi.gov or www.recreation.gov.

③. Best fishing holes

No really good fisherman worth his weight is going to let loose all those exact venues where the big ones never-ever get away —unless of course, you're visiting from overseas. Locals will oftentimes 'spill the beans' on best fishing spots because they know you'll not tell the entire neighborhood.

As far as fishing, we'll happily get you baited-up with a listing of the places we've been known to successfully drop a line or two in the drink. Go for it, the fishing is fine. I leave all my gear at home, opting to buy a new rod, reel, and tackle in the States as it saves me heaps, I add to my collection and I don't have to take

Cast off for America—you'll reel in a great holiday

Heat up the pan—dinner's on!

it along. Any large mega drug store, K Mart, Wal-Mart, Target, or other shop will sell the hardware and lures, my live baits I buy at the dock or local gas station on the day.

For more anglers' antics, try www.americasbestonline.net and ask about the fishing. We mentioned in another part of this book the fact that Americans seem to have a museum to cover almost any interest, and if you're ever near Manchester, (www.amff.com) Vermont, you can pop into the American Museum of Fly Fishing for a few tips.

Lake Mead, Nevada (it is very near Las Vegas) is chocker block full with striped bass. Other fish are few and far between but if you take light tackle you'll be kept very busy with reeling-cramp. Try www.travelnevada.com. Hire a houseboat for a few days and explore the lake, part of the Colorado River that has been backed up behind Hoover Dam and drop a line. The locals can tell you what you need at www.sevencrown.com.

The Florida Keys, Florida. Party boats (aka 'head boats') take anglers offshore for great fishing, or you can hire a sport fisherman for the tuna, marlin, and big game trophies, which are almost always 'tag and release' unless it's a record. Mangrove and 'flats' fishing for snook, bonefish and tarpon are also good in the keys. Cast off to www.fla-keys.com.

Montauk Point, Long Island NY Striped bass and bluefish can be had in abundance along the Atlantic seaboard. We've nailed bucketsful of flounder and fluke off the bottom with baits as well. Long Island Sound produces some wonderful catches. In freshwater, try upstate New York for the trout in the nearby Catskill Mountains (you'll need a freshwater fishing license here) on the Delaware and Beaverkill Rivers.

Fishing anywhere in the Rocky Mountain States is fine for freshwater fishing. Be sure to buy a licence.

The 'catch' is sometimes bigger than the kids

Almost everything in DC is free

4. Best free attractions

To re-engineer an old saying, 'some of the best things in life are free', in America there are literally hundreds, no thousands of attractions and venues that are 'on the house'. These venues and attractions will cost you zip, zero, nada, nothing and they are salt and peppered everywhere across the United States. Start with www.free-attractions.com/attractions.

Some of my personal favorites are:

- The Bellagio Fountain Show in Las Vegas
- The nightly pirate ships battling it out every 90 minutes in front of the Treasure Island casino
- The Circus Circus Casino which treats the kids to high wire and circus performances
- The Staten Island Ferry is free and offers the best views of the NY skyline, Statue of Liberty, Ellis Island, and New York's bustling harbor.

Be flexible—nothing on holiday is carved in stone

The urban openness of Central Park

- The New York Museum of Natural History (they might have a 'donations' bucket out)
- The nocturnal ranger's talk and bat 'tornado' at Carlsbad Caverns, New Mexico.
- All of the museums of the Washington DC Smithsonian Institute.
- West Point Military Museum and West Point, NY
- New York Central Park, the kids' zoo, rowboats on the lake, free concerts, and Shakespeare at the open-air Delacorte Theater, kite-flying, the shops, meadow softball, roller-blades biking, and people-watching.

5. Best time of day or night

This may be my own thing, but when I'm in the USA I try to make the most of it. If time is money, I'm always on the prowl to earn more.

Avoid rush hour like the plague; the locals have to suffer the traffic snarls, you don't.

The early bird catches the worm. I'm up early to be at the front of the line. Many major attractions now open their doors an hour before the general public is invited along, so check into VIP passes and pre-purchasing multi-day passes to get you inside before the hoards descend on the place.

If I've got long stretches of open road to cover, I prefer to drive late at night when there is less traffic and distraction.

Parks and monuments showcase American history for free

Pace yourself—it's a big place!

I'm not afraid to admit it, I love my midday naps when I'm on holiday. Find a bit of shade, curl up with a good book and decompress. Authorities on the subject say that taking a micro-nap (anything under 30 minutes) will keep you ticking longer and more alert to your surroundings. The Mexicans, Spaniards, and Portuguese have been doing their 'siesta' thing successfully for generations. Don't enforce a siesta on the crew, however, they may want to take the free time to re-dip in the pool, go shopping, take in a movie, or hire a bike.

I like to eat early, so I make reservations in advance, arrive on time and get the table and view I like and engage my waiter or waitress at the beginning of their shift and not when the joint becomes a mad-house. Your odds are very good that they'll still have plenty of the 'special of the day' on hand. When we eat early, I don't feel pressured to move along and we all enjoy the setting and our meal; after all, we're on vacation.

The beach is just as pleasant in the earlier part of the day before late-comers invade to stake a claim for beach blankets and volleyball. And I love taking ownership of the deckchairs at the pool in the late afternoon when other folks have sunned and swam and are already headed for home. Remember, America hosts 6 different times zones, observes daylight savings and in some cases, the locals or Native Americans run the place on their own time clock.

6. Best kitsch signs in the USA

Americans have a sense of humor when it comes to road signage, and you'll find yourself doing a double take on some of the more subtle examples. I'm often convinced the locals are just downright 'taking the mickey out' of passers-by. The top

Inter-galactic eateries—alien appetizers

list of these can be enjoyed at www.roadtripamerica.com, a collection of signs submitted by concerned citizens. Go ahead and pull over to take a snapshot if you come across one; they make great backdrops to your scrapbook and are a good conversation-starter anywhere you go.

Some of my all-time favorites are billboards like: A 'Used Cows' for sale sign in the American Midwest, or the sign in the coffee shop, which advises, 'Unattended children will be given an espresso and a free puppy!' There's also the sign at the precipice of a pit that proclaims: 'Bottomless Pit – 65 feet deep!' Or the tongue-firmly-in-cheek car wash signage that claims to give the 'Best Hand Job in Town!' Or the street sign for Cemetery Lane which is a 'Dead End'. Or the very official-looking sign in a national park that claims 'Toilet Room Ahead—No Dumping'.

For even more of these creative and sometimes confusing curbside advisories, try www.netscape.com and ask for unique road signs.

7. Best of the biggest

Americans have a real affinity for things BIG. In most of America, the bigger the better. When Americans have something special to shout about, they go to great lengths to enlarge it so there's no way other folks don't also get the message. If you just have to know before you go where the world's biggest yo-yo, hammer, pineapple, ball of barbed wire are, get super-sized and then some at www.worldslargestthings.com.

So to just name a few of my favorites here flies:

The world's largest Catsup bottle® stands proudly next to Route 159, just south of downtown Collinsville, Illinois. This unique 170-foot tower was built in 1949 by the W.E. Caldwell Company for the G.S. Suppiger catsup bottling plant. It actually doubles as

Gasoline is still cheaper in the USA and measured in gallons

a water tower for an entire township.

The biggest bison (or American buffalo) happens to be a massive concrete monster that watches over the entry to the National Buffalo Museum in Jamestown, North Dakota. The concrete creature is over 25 feet tall, but please don't take my word for it. Go and see the thing for yourself if you're in that part of the world. Try www.nationalbuffalomuseum.com.

If your launching pad for seeking out the 'Big stuff' in the USA starts in LA, you can make a full-on road tip of connecting the dots between big dinosaurs and donuts. America's largest permanent presentation of a donut is still the home of some great, if not a wee bit on the sugary side drive-thru donuts in Westchester California, within easy drive to Los Angeles International Airport. The massive 22-foot tall piece of pastry has a sign out front begging visitors to 'Eat Me!' And LA also boasts

Bigger is better in America

Eye-catching cattle

the world-renowned HOLLYWOOD hills sign, a massive chair outside of the Pacific Design Center, and across the road from the Sidewalk of the Stars, the Guinness Museum has an exact replica of the tallest man in the world. Venice Beach boasts a bodacious Barbell alongside Muscle Beach. While you're in the neighborhood, take a peek at the big binoculars on the binocular building outside the ad gurus' offices of Day/MOJO.

And please don't make a trip to the USA without a stopover in Darwin, Minnesota to see the worlds' largest ball of twine or to ogle at Minnesota's' rendering of Paul Bunyan and his best pet, Babe the Blue Ox, whose hoof prints are fabled to have stomped out the near 10,000 lakes on the state. Kim Whittaker of www.everywheremag.com did a great story on quirky and big-stuff in a Road Signs article. For a list of big things in the USA, try www.quirkylandmarks.com.

⑧. Best American diners

In the 1920s and 30s, travel by train was king. And it was considered every bit a big deal to eat aboard. Dining carriages had white-gloved waiters in black tie, wine lists, and even finger bowls to embellish a meal by rail. An 'upper crust' experience. Clever entrepreneurs, wanting to ring cash registers, picked up on this American longing, and begin designing and building eateries that resembled dining cars and carriages. The idea seems to be almost exclusively American and, although countless diners have fallen to the wreckers' ball, many remain as icons of the American landscape—with some new versions on an old theme popping into existence where it helped draw in diners to the diners. If the short-order cook whips up your platter in front of you, this is a good thing. Sometimes they sing a song as they sizzle.

Here are our best bites for dining, diner-style. You've got to try it at least once in America; sit at the counter and order a soda-pop, or take to a vinyl-covered booth and pop dimes into the table-side jukebox of rock and roll oldies but goldies. After all, you have to eat anyhow and this option is simply downright fun. Don't point if your waitress rocks up on roller-skates.

Although they're a clone of the original, **Lori's Diners** are all over San Francisco, and offer up great fun served at good value. Nail down the burgers with Idaho-sized French fries, a malted milkshake or a famous ice cream soda for yourself. Even if you've eaten at one Loris, try others as each one has different props, wall-hangings and authentic American 'pop artifacts'. Pre-peek at the menu at www.lorisdiner.com.

The Truckee Diner in Truckee, California sits on the railroad siding of this near Lake Tahoe township. It's aluminum-sided and well equipped to turn over some of the best club

Yummy in the tummy, with a cherry on top

sandwiches and pancakes in the county. Linger in the town too, it has old western boardwalks and store facades and good old western history to tell. Try: www.truckee.com.

Although not really in Brooklyn, the **Brooklyn Diner at Times Square in Manhattan** is great fun. Cheeky waiters and waitresses add to the NY flavor and Jewish, Italian, Irish, and other ethnic offerings sit well on the menu alongside more traditional fare. You can still go to the original site in Brooklyn, but Times Square is easier to access. See the menu at www. brooklyndiner.com. Listen carefully and practice your 'Neuw Uurk' accent here, the staff needs a good laugh.

Another franchise diner outfit is **Johnny Rockets Diner**, with locations sprinkled about the countryside and in urban areas. I like the ones in the Venetian Casino of Las Vegas and in the Hilton Hotel and casino in Reno, Nevada; both welcome the kids. The company hosts a countrywide list of locations to choose from; go to www.johnnyrockets.com.

Bobby's Big Boy of Burbank, California is one of the last free-standing, neon light bastions of hot rod cult and big hand-crafted hamburgers. You may find celebrities taking aboard cholesterol count at the counter seats—the place has been used as a set for many a Hollywood period flick and the food is fine 24 hours a day, every day of the year. Locals still 'burn rubber' in the palm-lined parking lot. Try www.bigboy.com.

Mel's' Drive-in in Sherman Oaks California is an all-aluminum (The Americans pronounce this word very differently than you) aircraft fuselage architecture of the earlier 'American Graffiti' era. They don't stay open 24 hours any more but you can still have late-night cops on the beat, drinking caffeine at the counter. Try www.melsdrive-in.com.

The iconic other **Mel's is on Sunset Blvd** in West Hollywood and stays open around the clock and is a great late-night celeb-spotting venue. While you are waiting for your order, check out the wall hangings and fellow revelers who just might be nocturnal animals of some notoriety. Mel's places cover the landscape in California, with themes and menus similar to the 'originals' and you can find them on the company website at www.melsdrive-in.com.

Mickey's Diner in St Paul Minnesota has been made famous as a backdrop for a few Midwestern film shoots and still manages to serve up great nostalgia and a nice stack of pancakes. Big on midwest value for your eating dollar, they still do the milkshakes and malts by hand. Look over the menu before placing your order at www.mickeysdiningcar.com. Even if you never wind up in St Paul, check the place out on the net —it has been used in many a movie.

For more of the roadside eats in America, park yourself at www.themaiericanroadside.com as they have oodles and oodles of great roadside eats for the asking.

9. Best museums

If you've got an interest, Americans appear to have a museum to match it, and then some. From firearms to barbed wire fencing, from bottle caps to knives, automobiles and bikes to interplanetary aliens and Elvis. America is an entire treasure chest of brilliant museums to tempt you. To list all our own favorites would require knocking down far too many trees. Meander to some of Americas' museum sites for yourself on www.museumca.org.

My all-time favorite is the **Buffalo Bill Museum** in Cody, Wyoming. Absolutely the bees-knees for western history, Native American cultures, firearms of the old west, and much, much more. Six monster museums all under one timber roof. The museum shares its backyard with the Grand Teton Mountains. An added bonus is the world-class rodeo. Saddle-up and see for yourself at www.bbhc.org.

Mystic Seaport Museum in Mystic Connecticut. Without a doubt this place has the lure of the sea, with significant ships that visitors can clamor aboard. Take good walking shoes, it's a big place. To fully peek ahead onto the pier cast a line to www.mystic.org.

ZEUM in San Francisco. The ZEUM museum is totally hands on for all ages; kids let creative juices flow, make 30-second commercials, create behind the cameras, and it is 'totally fun' for everyone. Try www.zeum.org and while you are in San Francisco, don't miss touching everything hands-on in the Exploratorium at www.exploratorium.edu.

The Autry National Museum, Griffith Park Los Angeles CA. Tucked into mammoth Griffith Park, this museum is exceptional value. An excellent collection of western artifacts and displays, it is a great place for all ages; it looks at Hollywood 'westerns' from both sides of the tee-pee. Put on the spurs and trot to www.autry-museum.org and when you're finished, try some horseback riding at the nearby hire stables in the park.

Colonial Williamsburg, Virginia. Funds from the well-heeled Rockefeller family fortunes made this place a living history book. An entire town of Williamsburg, complete with butter-makers, bakers, and candlestick makers who daily turn back the clock to life as it was lived during the colonial period in American history. If you're staying in Washington DC leave for Williamsburg early as you'll need a full day here. You can walk onto the site for free, but narrated tours and guides are the go—you'll learn so much more from hearing it as well as seeing it. Turn back the clock and try www.history.org. If you still have time on your hands, go to Jamestown Landing in the same area, see the three replica ships—the Nina, the Pinta, and the Santa Maria and take the free car ferry over the James River to 'Sydney'. No passort required.

Museum of Modern Art, New York City. Known as MoMA to locals, this is the depository of some huge pieces, Picasso and Dali to name-drop only a pair.

Fantastic, so be sure to go to www.moma.org. Buy a CityPass™ and you're in. I love the gift shops and coffee venues in the museums; you meet the nicest people there.

Arizona Sonora Desert Museum in Tucson, Arizona. This is one of the very best living museums and eye-to-eye zoos in the entire country. The landscape, animal habitats, and the setting is what hundreds of westerns are made of. Home of giant sequoia cactus and others, this is a few minutes out of town yet light years away to some honestly excellent exhibits. Try www. desertmuseum.org.

The Polynesian Cultural Center is about an hour's drive from Waikiki Beach and boasts exhibits and hands-on activities for absolutely everyone; learn to light fires, play the ukulele like a local, home in on your hula dancing and be sure to stay on for the luau and evening showcase. Not cheap but an excellent full day outing—educational, fun and enlightening. Go to www.polynesia.com.

The National Air and Space Museum Washington DC Mall is free and you can fly a flight-simulator, kick the tires on the moon-mobile, watch the IMAX 'Hail Columbia' film and more. Pace yourselves, its massive and only one of many buildings of the Smithsonian Institute. Try www.nasa.gov.

Alcatraz, San Francisco Bay, California gets thousands of visitors each year, and has become so popular that you need to pre-book, sometimes days if not weeks in advance, to get a place on the ferry. Other cruise companies can take you around the infamous 'rock' but only the designated ferry company makes scheduled visits to the one-time prison block, home to

Local events are often free. You're invited to try too!

some of the FBI's most wanted. Go to www.alcatrazcruises.com for the low-down on the lock-up.

Guggenheim Museum, New York City. Designed by Frank Lloyd Wright, the building is a corkscrew of the world's finest art. Take the elevator to the top and just start meandering your way south to the lobby. Not to be missed with a CityPass™. Try www.guggenheim.org and www.citypass.com.

The Getty Museum, Los Angeles is a massive gift to the American people from the very well-heeled J. Paul Getty family. The collection is extensive, entry is free but you must pre-book a place or you'll never get past security at the main gate. It's well worth the effort to see some of the world's finest art treasures. Try www.getty.edu.

The Chicago Museum of Sciences, Chicago, Illinois, said to be the largest science museum in the western hemisphere, has a 'working coal mine' in the basement and a captured German sub from World War II. The place is loaded with great, interactive activities for all ages. Try www.msichicago.org.

10. Best national parks and natural wonders

Wilderness is not a luxury but a necessity of the human spirit.
Edward Abbey

To list all of the wonderful parks and reserves would require volumes. So I've short-listed just a few of my own favorites of those 'must-see sites' to target as you plan your holiday in the USA. The list is in no particular order, as they're all brilliant. Don't be discouraged if you can't get to them all in one go. It takes the Americans a lifetime and then some to cover even the top 10. You'll just have another good reason for returning! For overall good information on the national parks system in the USA try www.nps.gov. If you're trekking around America and taking in more than one national park, buy yourself an annual pass and you'll wind up saving money. One thing we know is certain, any trip to the USA without making a visit to one of its magnificent National Parks would be nothing short of a real pity. Grab yourself a National Parks Pass and remember to 'take only photographs, and leave only footprints'. Hopefully someone will follow in your footsteps three, four, or five generations from now.

Yosemite National Park, California

Practice pronouncing this one in front of the mirror, 'Yo-SEM-It-eee', which is an Indian word for the 'place of many bears'.

Other nationalities love referring to Yosemite National Park as 'YO-ZEE-MITE, a natural hiccup based on the spelling of the national eating icons—Vegemite or Marmite.

No matter how you care to pronounce it, Yosemite is home to waterfalls 7 times higher than the raging waters of Niagara, over 750 miles of wilderness trails, abundant bears and, as though this wasn't enough to make it the most visited of all the national parks in the USA, Yosemite is home to the oldest living things on the planet Earth. The giant redwoods and sequoias, many of them weighing in at over 3,000 years of age and counting. That's 1000 years before the birth of Christ.

Standing among these gentle giants is an experience very few will forget. Visitors can fish for trout in the crystal-clear waters, or refresh themselves by jumping (carefully please) from any number of bridges along the Merced River, or 'inner tube' lazily along in the Yosemite Valley.

'Yosemite' is an Indian word meaning 'the place of many bears'

If you're inclined to climb, El Captain and Half Dome Granite monoliths are a hiker's dream come true. You can hire bikes or horses, or simply avail yourself to the free and environmentally friendly trams that ply the park. The wildlife, not threatened by hunting, is 'very friendly' and heavy fines are imposed for feeding or leaving food where the bears and other wildlife can get them. The park is very, very popular so plan in advance. Local information is best from www.yosemite.national-park. com.

Yellowstone, Wyoming

Try not to depart the planet without visiting America's first National Park, Yellowstone. The park size-wise is three times the state of Rhode Island, or 2,219,789 acres or, to put it in off-shore terms, almost 9,000 square kilometers. The locals are not inclined to brag and tend to downplay the natural attractions but the fact is, Yellowstone is marvelous.

Yellowstone boasts some wonderful, and sometimes overly enthusiastic wildlife. Free-roaming buffalo (aka bison) roam in significant herds, massive moose, elk, grey wolves, grizzly and black bear, bighorn sheep, the bald eagle, coyote, mountain lion, and others live without fear of the hunter's rifle.

Yellowstone is also home to 'the Ole Faithful' geyser, neighboring inside the parks' boundaries with more than 10,000 other thermal features, including geysers, steam vents, hot springs, and colorful thermal pools. Hiking, horseback riding, river 'floating', camping under canvas, and basking in the hot-springs are all just samples of how visitors enjoy the natural settings. The animals have the right of way with signs alerting drivers to 'Please Break for Bears!' and 'Bears Crossing!' For onsite information on the park and its surrounding areas try www.yellowstone.net.

If a bear wants your lunch ... give it to him

The Grand Canyon, Arizona

Surrounded by the Hualapai, Havasupai and Navajo tribal lands, the Grand Canyon almost defies description, although thousands of scribes who were far better equipped than this writer have tried. The rim trails of this magnificent marvel of Mother Nature are 7,000 feet above sea level, and the drop from the south rim is a mile straight down to the Colorado River.

The colors and temperament of the canyon can change like the snap of your fingers: one minute it is rosy crimson, baked in sunlight and the next, it is rainbow-covered with jet-black sheets of rain or snow which can be seen 100 miles off to the horizon. Important things to keep in mind when planning a trip here are that the place can be below freezing temperatures at night, to reaching over 40 degrees by high noon at certain times of the year. Being at 7,000 feet above sea level, the sun's burning rays have 35% more parching-power than at the ocean's edge—any many visitors don't cover up properly, or take enough water along. There are trails to the bottom, that, although only 16 to 18 miles round-trip, take an entire day and you need to be in fit fiddle to tackle them. For most, just a short walk down a few miles and back is sufficient, and trail walks along the canyon rim are spectacular and lined with informative guideposts and observation points. Try and take in a sunset or sunrise, and invest in the IMAX film outside the south gates of the park, which is a brilliant introduction. Also at the South Entrance you'll find horseback hire, helicopter flight-seeing, sure-footed Mule treks, and white-water rafting on the Colorado River, which can also be booked from the South entrance. Try www.explorethecanyon.com.

Sunset or sunrise—it's always amazing

Simply ask. Everyone's eager to assist.

What to do, how to get around there, nightlife and wildlife and what's available just outside the official gates can be found at www.nps.gov/grca.

Monument Valley, Navajo National Reservation, Utah

Known among the Navajo as 'The Valley of Rocks', Monument Valley is nothing short of spectacular.

The surrounding area is also referred to as 'the Valley of the Gods', and is home to ancient cliff dwellings and ancient rock art.

Monument Valley has been the backdrop for over 300 western movies and has come to symbolise the 'old west' for an entire generation of movie-goers. A Navajo-inspired guide to the Valley is a 'must'.

Bryce Canyon and Zion Canyon National Parks, Utah

Like two Siamese twins joined together at the ankle, Bryce and Zion parks are two very different siblings, sharing the same bedroom. But it would be unfair to speak about one and not the other because over 99% of the visitation to one, makes it a must to pass thru the other.

Bryce Canyon, according to Ebenezer Bryce himself, was referred to as 'a hell of a place to lose a cow!' After you've visited you can fully appreciate the old boys' comments. The Piute Indians used Bryce for religious purposes and attributed to it, supernatural powers. They called it 'red rocks standing like men'. Colors are magnificent, and visitors can hike among giant chess pieces, carved by erosion, wind, and weather. The best site is still the one launched by the National Park Service at www.

Get a stranger to take the shot and make a friend in the process

Homes take on many shapes in the States

nps.gov/bryce. Beds and campsites inside the park are often over taxed but nearby Ruby's Inn takes all the overflow with a grin. Try www.rubysinn.com.

Zion National Park was carved some 200 million years ago by the hand and imagination of mother nature. During the Depression, national work corps teams carved extensive tunnels thru the mountains to access the more remote areas and oddly shaped formations, such as 'frog getting ready to jump' , 'checkerboard mesa', or 'the spear-chucker', are only a few of the parks' natural attractions. Try www.nps.gov/zion.

The Badlands, South Dakota

Boasting over 240,000 acres and significant fossil finds dating back some 35 million years ago, the mixed-grass prairie lands of the Badlands got their name from the plains Indians. Indians and later-day pioneers referred to the area as 'maco sica' or 'lands bad'. Estimates suggest that over 60 million buffalo roamed this prairie long after saber-toothed tigers, three-toed horses and humpless camels grazed on the site. Because of no real light pollution, the area offers some of the best and unobstructed star-gazing anywhere in America. This area is shrouded by Indian reservations with names like Cactus Flat, Red Shirt, and Wounded Knee and has been the backdrop for many a Hollywood western. Try www.nps.gov/badlands. Nowadays, there are so many good reasons to visit the Badlands.

Death Valley, California

Not only is Death Valley the driest and hottest place in the USA, with temperatures rising above 120 degrees Fahrenheit in the shade, but it is also the lowest point in the continental USA, some 300 feet below sea level. The Indians referred to the valley as

Local traffic conjestion—not!

'Tomsha' meaning, 'ground afire'. Scotties Castle is only one of the area's calling cards, a castle created by an old mining geezer who prospected the area.

Death Valley holds the USA record for the hottest day ever recorded; a whopping 134 degrees Fahrenheit. There are many breathtaking beautiful places, ghost towns, and oases in Death Valley, such as Devils Golf Course, Hells Gate, and Furnace Creek. For stargazing, the lack of visual and light pollution inside the 3,000 square miles of its boundaries put Death Valley at the top of the alien's lookout list. Bring Water and top up the fuel tank before lighting out! Try www.nps.gov.

Niagara Falls, New York

A massive 750,000 gallons pour over the falls every second. And for most visitors, just standing at the railing on the US or Canadian side of the falls is sufficient. Other more-adventuresome types tried to gain notoriety by going over the raging waters in wooden barrels, life-jackets or home-made contraptions and you can view their remnants at near-by museums. Thousands of international visitors walk across the Peace Bridge to Canada annually and if you do the crossing, be certain beforehand that your visa and passport papers are in order and on-hand. If you plan to get wet, the 'Maid of the Mist' boats have been specially designed with this purpose in mind. The price of admission includes the loan of a rain jacket and the cruise nuzzles right up to the spray-line. If you want to tackle the falls on foot, you can join a behind the torrent, screen of water tour into the 'Cavern of the Winds'. A word of warning: some visitors are fussed over the commercial sites that trim this natural wonder; museums with artifacts and body-parts of those who tried to go over the raging torrent in barrels, other 'believe it or not' museums line the boulevards on either side of the falls. Hotels, B&B, curio shops,

750,000 gallons a second and counting

and eateries line the walkways. Local information is available from www.niagara-usa.com.

I think having land and not ruining it is the most beautiful art that anybody could ever want to own.
Andy Warhol

11. Best of musical America

From jazz legends to Elvis, to rock and roll and country and western, Americans have plenty of time for a tune or two. Even if you're not musically inclined, America has conjured up a lyric line that tickles many a nerve, unlocks emotions and gets the toes tapping. While in America, strum up a cord or two and hum a few bars; even if it is out of tune, and only in the shower.

Year-round Americans are entertained with live music offerings, many of which are free of charge, and open air events. Search for annual musical events on line as the listing seems almost endless. Our top pick of musical places is only the tip of the tunes.

Radio City Music Hall in New York City. With its marquee an entire block long, and 300 million paying customers to its credit, Radio City Music Hall is a must for the Manhattan visit. The venue boasts world class entertainment in the largest indoor theater in the world. The art deco design was the brain child of millionaire John D. Rockefeller, who invested over 90 million dollars during the Depression. Even if you don't buy tickets to a show, go there. Try www.radiocity.com.

Country Music Hall of Fame and Museum in Nashville Tennessee's Music Row will set your toes tapping, even if you're not a country and western aficionado. From Elvis' Cadillac and costumes to Willy Nelson's guitars, this venue holds the

Just do it! You only go around once. Think of the bragging rights.

Musical America—belting out the blues

crown jewels of country music. Cut your own demo tape in Studio B, the same venue for legends like Elvis. Try www.countrymusichalloffame.com.

Rock and Roll Museum in Cleveland, Ohio lures millions of guests annually to its reverberating doors on the shores of Lake Erie. From Ray Charles to Jethro Tull, the Moody Blues to BB King and The Animals this is a great venue. Exhibits and events change at high volume here so check ahead and grab tickets. Try www.rockhall.com.

'Graceland' in Memphis, Tennessee was the home of Elvis Presley, the undisputed ' king of rock and roll', and is open to the public and well worth the trip. The guy might not have had a flair for interior decoration—wait till you see the 'safari room'—but he could shake it up and belt out a tune like nobody's business. Across the road you can clamber aboard Elvis' private jet and step into his blue seude shoes. www.elvis.com.

Also in Memphis, 'Soulville' to be exact is the STAX Museum dedicated to American Soul Music and the one-time home of STAX Records and recording studios. From Otis Redding to the Staple Sisters and beyond, the legendary 'label' produced over 150 songs in the top 100 list. Try www.staxmuseum.com.

Motown Records and Museum in Detroit, Michigan is the mother lode. 'Hitsville USA' was the home of the Motown sound and the label's successful tracks and hits made it the largest independent recording studio in the world. Go into Studio A and the echo chamber and cut a few tracks of your own.

Sing along—even if you don't know all the words

The place produced hundreds of legendary greats. Try www. motownmuseum.com.

Preservation Hall in The French Quarter, New Orleans is located on Peter Street, only a few blocks from the Mississippi River and is host to nightly veterans of jazz, many ticking the timer in their 70s and 80s. Grab yourself a legendary Hurricane cocktail and pull up a seat. Be early, the place was once a private residence, so its very intimate. Stand in the street and listen-in like the locals. If music is your thing, you'll love Bourbon Street in the French Quarter. On any given night, you'll have a mixed menu of music at your ear-tips within the length of a football field from country western to jazz, progressive jazz, street musings, folk, classical, rock and roll, rockabilly, and more. Pubs, speakeasy-type venues, and saloons line the sidewalks and revelers take over the streets. Try www.preservationhall.com. While in New Orleans, visit the State Museum, which has a Jazz Museum as part of the permanent exhibit with iconic items from Louis Armstrong, Cab Calloway, and Duke Ellington, and the original Dixieland Jazz Band just to name drop a few.

Carnegie Hall in Manhattan was built in the late 1880s with money from the very well-heeled Andrew Carnegie. It boasts incredible acoustics and host the world's best in classical and modern music. From Bernstein to the Beatles and from black tie events to bluegrass and blue jeans, check to see what's on when you're in the Big Apple. Try www.carnegiehall.org. If you don't buy tickets, take the tour.

The Hollywood Bowl in Los Angeles California has hosted the lot. From the Beachboys to Bach's Best. Grab tickets, check out the website for freebies, on-the-house sessions, and jams and take a narrated tour at www.hollywoodbowl.com.

12. Best road trips

A great road trip in the USA can be a few hours long, or take weeks to accomplish. Major American motoring organizations, car clubs, Recreational Vehicle clubs, and others list their best of the blacktop offerings so we recommend you sit down at the kitchen table, open up the map, and start planning. You have about 7.4 million miles of roadway to choose from. Try www.aaa.com. The American Automobile Association is a membership group which, as part of its member benefits, produces a 'TripTik' of journeys and suggested attractions en route but plenty of information is available for free.

Travel wholesalers also develop fully packaged deals that include the car, the accommodation, and road notes to see

The call of the open road

you through with ease. These packages, known as 'Fly-Drive' programs, are available in many mainstream travel brochures. Try www.ati.com or www.driveaway.com for more details.

San Francisco to San Diego along the Pacific Coast Highway. This paved pearl necklace runs north to south along the California coastline and is chocker block with places, attractions, natural and man-made wonders. One of America's best-traveled pieces of pavement, Highway 1 and 101 has got to be one of the most popular road trips in the world. The hardest part is determining how many days you'll need to get from one end to the other. To list all the great vistas, attractions and stopovers could fill a book and this road trip can be custom-built to your own designs. Just stay focused on what you want and let the diversions reveal themselves as you drive along. Hidden treasures along this route are abundant. Try www.roadtrip.com.

Sonoma and Napa Valley Wine and Mine trip. Most road warriors start this trip crossing the Golden Gate Bridge and a stop-off at the 3,000-year-old trees of Muir Woods. The route takes you to some of America's best vineyards, all of whom offer free samples and tastings. And while in the area, you'll be privy to some of the surrounding 'gold rush' history that opened up the American West. www.fretrip.com is a site that lets you pick the slow and easy route, or the whiplash version.

Fall Foliage trip in New England. You'll need to be ready for fall foliage, which places you somewhat at the mercy of mother nature. Leaves begin to change color in the New England states after the first cold 'snap' and the window runs perhaps 8 weeks all-up. Late September till mid November is a safe bet, especially if you are free to move around from state to state for the best autumn colors. Don't overlook the lighthouses and lobsters, clam chowders, and excellent out of doors. Try www.gonewengland.about.com. For our money, make the most of it by adding the covered bridges of Vermont, made famous by the Clint Eastwood film, The Bridges of Madison County. Try www.vermontbridges.com.

From Miami to the Key West, Florida. Although this road trip is only about 150 miles long, don't assume you'll do it in a few hours. For one thing, it passes through some wonderful islands with many coral keys and sandy atolls, en route to Hemmingway's old haunts in Key West. And for another, its oftentimes only one lane going and one lane coming. Stop to swim, snorkel, fish, and sail. If you're not interested in water-oriented holidays, you'll still enjoy the nightly street festivals and watching sunsets at Mallory's Wharf, or peeking in on places of literary legends like Ernest Hemmingway and Tennessee Williams, or eating out and clubbing along the way. If you're behind a whopping big RV, be patient. Locals travel by flip-flop and 'conk bicycles'. Rent one and stay a while. Go to www.fla-keys.com.

Known as the 'Mother Road', Historic Route 66 from Chicago to Santa Monica, California is today made up of numerous other road numbers. Yet the sprit of the open road lives on. But you can still, as the song lyrics say: 'Travel my way, the highway that's the best. Get your kicks on Route 66!' Take the Route 66 trivia test, slow down the pace, and see if you can connect all the ancient gas pumps, diners, and pit stops that made the roadway famous. Drive fast to www.historic66.com.

The Blue Ridge Parkway, Virginia. Leave it to American ingenuity to build 105 miles of roadway along the backbone of the Blue Ridge Mountains. The scenic roadway was built by the Depression-era Civilian Conservation Corps and no matter which way you turn, the view is spectacular. The National Park Service calls this high-in-the-sky roadway, Skyline Drive. Try www.nps.com. Pullouts and stone walls line the drive and the visitor center has all the history of the flora, fauna, and how it all

Celebrate the differences in landscapes and locals

Our suggested road trips are only intended to get your motor going. Over 100 sites and thousands of blogs address the best roadway revelations and we share the thoughts of author, Least Heat Moon's journey into America in Blue Highways. He is convinced that the road less traveled offers the best of America.

For more on the best road trips in and around the USA, try www.shermanstravel.com or www.holidaysonsale.com.

13. Best shopping malls and discounts

Shopping in America has for many years been number one on most international visitors' list of activities, and for very good reason. Americans themselves love to shop, and have paved the way for massive discount shopping centers, factory outlets, strip centers and mega shopping malls. Department stores such as Macy's and Bloomingdale's take up entire city blocks. Parents' rooms, child care, even pre-schools, amusement parks, libraries, and other community services have all been joined together under one roof for the sole purpose of seducing consumers and ringing cash registers. We love every bit of it! Once you've established the region you'll be visiting in the USA, get cracking. Nail down the shopping that suits your need to fill up the suitcases, buy the gifts for those left behind, and stock up on items you simply can't live without. The really amazing thing about America's malls is that they only started to show up on the American landscape in the 1950s. Before that, all the good shopping was along 'Main Street' in towns and cities. If you are keen to see some vintage photos of the earlier malls go onto www.mallsofamerica.blogspot.com. Shopping at a mall has become a social event, which includes dining, entertainment, people-watching, socializing, and more today. Make the most

Texas two-stepping—try these on for size

of it. Start off looking for the bargains and outlet malls, of which there are hundreds. Push your shopping cart to www. outletbound.com for a partial list of places near you. Of the 225 listed and large outlet malls in the USA, the take is over $12 billion so they must be offering good value or the Americans wouldn't be shopping in them. Another great way to pre-plan your spending is to look over the in-line shops and 'anchor' tenants of major shopping malls before actually rocking up to the parking lot. This has been made easy by pre-peeking at malls in the Shop America Alliance. Go to www.shopamericavip.com.

The all-time big mamma of malls has got to be the Mall of America in Minnesota. This place redefines the term massive. Just to throw a bit of Mall of America trivia at you, did you know that: The mall cost over $650 million to build, boasts over 14 movie

Extraordinary eats and festive feasts

screens, can accommodate 7 Yankee Stadiums, 32 Boeing 747s, employs over 11,000 people, and has an entire amusement park under its roof. The roller coaster is a doozie. Even if you never get there in the flesh to flex your credit cards, visit on line at www. mallofamerica.com.

My all-time favorite is Macy's, simply because the staff knows the stock from department to department, and, more importantly, they'll hand over to any international visitor smart enough to show a license or passport, a deep-pocket discount card on the spot. This card is HUGE because it gives international shoppers a whopping 11% off of almost anything, including items that have already been placed on sale at 75% off. This card is not available to the Americans and you'll need to show ID to get one. And there is no limit to the damage you can do to the credit cards as far as Macy's is concerned. Get ready, get set, get shopping at www.macys.com.

Being a bargain hunter, I also look for free-standing stores that proclaim the 'never pay full price' like Marshals, Big Lots, Sam's Club, Target, Wal-Mart, TJ Max and Odd Lots. On occasion I've returned home with an item that prompts me to dig up a quote from the English essayist, John Ruskin, who wrote:

It's unwise to pay too much but it's unwise to pay too little. When you pay too much, you lose a little money, that is all. But when you pay too little, you sometimes lose everything. Because the thing you bought was incapable of doing the thing that you bought it to do.

In these venues, it's possible to get some great deals, but you need to look over goods carefully. Some may offer brand name 'seconds' with little or no apparent blemishes or defects, while other items might have major trauma to tackle.

14. Best ski areas

We're bound to tick someone off with this list because the best skiing in the USA is a matter of personal preference. One thing is certain, there is a great deal of 'loyalty' attached to ski areas, and there is no shortage of variety in choosing a place to suit your snowboarding or skiing wish list. Here's an abbreviated list but do go to the experts on your own to select the best go in the snow for your trip. Dress warmly. I like Powder Magazine at www.powdermag.com for all the up-to-date on the white stuff. Go onto www.isubscribe.com and land yourself a great subscription for titles snow-related. While you're there pick out a few American motoring magazines as well.

Park City, Utah is a young, talented and on-the-wild side. crowd. Après Ski is tops for late-night owling and the snow is powder dry and plentiful. Try www.parkcityinfo.com.

Jackson Hole, Wyoming I love Jackson Hole, home of the one-time bad boys, the Hole-in-the-Wall gang and today home to many celebrities who ranch in the area, such as Harrison Ford. Home to some great lifts, the Million Dollar Cowboy bar where skiers sidle up to the bar on real Western saddles. Test the slopes by day, and mechanical bulls by night. Snowboarding is big in Grand Teton town. Try www.www.jacksonhole.com.

Aspen and Vail in Colorado are the 'in spots' for anyone wanting to ski and see. Winter wardrobes, both on and off the slopes are significant and so is the snow.

There is plenty of variety in lifts, runs, and slopes, but bring your credit card along. Star-spotters beware; this is possibly America's best place to snow-plow alongside the rich and famous. For the lowdown on the two locations go to www.coloradoski.com and check out your local tour operators who specialise in ski holidays as they often have packages that beat buying in bits and pieces.

Snow central

Spectacular snow

Sugarloaf, Maine and Stowe, Vermont are among the best-known and equipped slopes on the eastern seaboard of the USA. If you're gateway city in winter is New York or Boston, these slopes make perfect dollars and cents. Otherwise, bite the bullet and head west. Go to www.sugarloaf.com and compare local price packages or www.stowe.com for great photos and hourly updates on conditions in winter. Both of these venues are great outdoors all-year round.

Lake Tahoe, Nevada, and California for my money, this region has a tremendous variety of ski and snowboarding options for everyone. The hardest part is selecting which area to take on, as Squaw Valley, Diamond Peak, Heavenly, Mt. Rose, and a dozen other great slopes are all within a one-hour drive of the lake or less. For ski-in and ski-out it'd have to be Squaw but shop around, they all offer multi-day passes and some require more ski abilities than others. Try www.skilaketahoe.com and www. laketahoeskiing.com, which are two great places to get started. Remember, you can ski in two states here, some trails crossing state lines between Nevada and California. They gamble on

Eat, drink and be 'ski'

the Nevada side and California is a smoke-free state.

15. Best unusual place names

Americans have a sense of humor, optimism, and adventure when it comes to place names. Towns like 'YumTum, Coffee City, Hungry Horse, Grey Mule, and literally thousands of other places are worthy of mention. Some town fathers are reconsidering their municipal 'monikers' as we write, but try for a partial listing of the lyrical landscapes of the USA at www.accuracyproject. org/towns.

Here is a partial listing of places for your perusal. Thinking naughty? How about:

Hope and Consequences, New Mexico

Sweet Lips, Tennessee

Fanny, West Virginia

Busti, New York

Bird in Hand, Pennsylvania

Big Beaver, Pennsylvania

Butts, Georgia

Buttzville, New Jersey

Dicktown, New Jersey

Erect, North Carolina

New Erection, Virginia

Dickshooter, Idaho

Intercourse, Pennsylvania

Loving, New Mexico

Climax, Georgia

Virgin, Utah

Conception, Missouri

Fidelity, Missouri

17. Best recommended reading

Library on wheels

Almost anywhere in America, folks are prepared to swap one good read for another; coffee shops, gas stations, hotel lobbies, campgrounds, and others will have a mini-library of books that have been already read, and are ready to pass along as a swap to anyone who wishes. I've grabbed some of my very best reads this way and you can rest assured they've had a fair bit of mileage on them, but nobody cares. Read on, and pass your yarns onto someone else. It's very nice to share.

Reading up before you take off for the USA is also a great way to extend the excitement of your visit. Pop into the local library, tap your friends on the shoulder for titles they've enjoyed, scour the book sales, and begin gearing up for the holiday of a lifetime in America. Enjoy yourself for hours, days, weeks, and even months before you go along to the USA with some good reading.

This is just my list of favorites. Ask around and you'll very quickly discover mine is only a drop in the pond of the good reading available on America. Do drop us a line if you uncover a personal favorite—we're always interested in a good book and a good read. Go to www.overeasyguides.com.

Don't forget to read up via the American magazines and newspapers as well, many of them available on-line. Buy a few of the ones you like from: www.isubscribe.com.

Working—Studs Terrell
On The Road—Jack Kerouac
America—John Dos Passes
The Americans—Henry James
Americans—Alistair Cooke

Follow the signs

Coping With America—Peter Trudge
Trout-Fishing In America—Richard Rattigan
Leaves of Grass—Walt Whitman
Centennial—James A Michener
The Making Of America—BW Bancroft
Blue Highways—Least Heat Moon
Travels With Charley—John Steinbeck
Cannery Row—John Steinbeck
Home Country—Ernie Pyle
Any 'Eyewitness' Travel Guide
Desert Solitaire—Edward Abbey
Walk In the Woods—Bill Bryson
Made in America—Bill Bryson

18. Best celebrity spotting

In the USA, professional photographers and the 'paparazzi' pack get there first, so don't try too hard. Let them come to you. For our money, just plant yourself in a place you like, and wait for the talent to pass you by. Best cities for celebrity spotting are still the major areas of entertainment like LA and New York where the law of averages are in your favor. Park yourself poolside at a well-known Hollywood or Beverly Hills hotel and you're got a good chance someone of note will turn up. Go to www.seeing-stars.com for the inside skinny and remember to check the local rags and periodicals for openings, premieres, and special events that will attract the talent. Going to staging areas and on location filming sites is another surefire way to get a peek. Grab www.variety.com, the entertainment industry's daily sheet on the stars and casting calls. If you hang out at the backstage door of venues like the Ed Sullivan Theater in New York, you're going to see the likes of David Letterman and his guests, even if its only a cameo appearance. And populating the better hotels, restaurants, and clubs where the well-heeled and well-known frequent, improves your odds considerably. Get tickets to be in the audience of TV programs like Oprah, Jay Leno, or Late Night with David Letterman, which are almost always free tickets to a handshake or two.

Window shop along Fifth Avenue in New York and Rodeo Drive in Beverly Hills. With a day in either place, you're guaranteed to spot someone on the A-list.

Visit one of the trendy gyms for a workout; even if you have the money for a private trainer, you still make the scene at the gym. Working out while you're waiting is also a good

The welcome mat is out—come on over!

thing, even if nobody turns up. Try www.losangeles.citysearch. com, which does a great listing of where to hang out to spot the celebs and the West Hollywood Visitors and Convention Authority has the top 101 places that lure the stars. Try www.visitwesthollywood.com.

It's a Wrap!

It's a bit like the old proverb, you can lead a horse to water but you can't make it drink. We're tried our hardest here to lay down some of the juicy bits and motivate you to get started. Remember to use your accent, relax, and take it all in. America and the Americans will inspire, entertain, and enlighten you in ways you never dreamed possible. The planning of an American getaway is good fun unto itself. Good luck with it all, and please, don't remain strangers; we'd love nothing more than to do another run of this title, which includes feedback from other folks. Toss your discoveries onto the pile of helpful hints alongside us. Our doors are always open electronically so please feel free to 'knock us up' (means get us pregnant in the USA) any time you like on www.overeasyguides.com.

Our Internet Index

Doing Your Homework! Before You Go!

We've tried to make it easy for you here, to simply 'move the mouse around' when making your plans for a great trip to the USA. So we've listed the most widely sought after sites, alongside our 'favorites' but this doesn't mean there are not thousands of others to consider! The book would never be big enough for them all!

When you've got all the 'must have' pieces in place, simply march into your local travel agent with your travel dates and wish-list in hand, and cut them loose to book it!

Our team has tested every attraction, site and activity listed here, and we can vouch for them all! Happy travels from The 'Over Easy!' team!

Get Started! Brand USA www.discoveramerica.com/
Writing US? www.overeasyguides.com

Tickets & Attractions

City Pass www.citypass.com
StubHub www.stubhub.com
Dig This! Las Vegas www.digthisvegas.com
Helicopter Flights NY www.heliny.com
New York Water Taxi www.nywatertaxi.com
Knottsbury Farm https://www.knotts.com/
Disneyland http://gocalifornia.about.com/cs/disneyland/a/disintro.htm
Universal Studios http://gocalifornia.about.com/cs/losangeles/a/universal.htm
New York Double Decker Bus Tours www.gonytours.com
Disneyworld https://disneyworld.disney.go.com/destinations/magic-

kingdom

Seaworld Parks http://seaworld.com/

Sonora Desert Museum, Arizona www.desertmuseum.org

Cody Nite Rodeo, Wyoming www.codynightrodeo.com

Buffalo Bill Historical Center, Cody, Wyoming http://centerofthewest.org

City of Deadwood Attractions www.cityofdeadwood.com

Hollywood www.hollywood.com

The Wheel America

Alamo Cars www.alamo.com/en_US/car-rental/home.html

El Monte Recreational Vehicles www.elmonterv.com

NY Limos www.dial7.com

LuxBusAmerica www.luxbusamerica.com

EagleRider Motorcycles www.eagleridger.com

The Must See Places & State Bureaus

The 'Real America' Rocky Mtn States www.rmi-realamerica.com/

Montana www.visitmt.com

Idaho www.visitidaho.com

Wyoming www.wyomingtourism.org

South Dakota www.travelsd.com

North Dakota www.ndtourism.com

California Tourism www.visitcalifornia.com/

San Francisco www.sanfrancisco.travel/

Santa Barbara www.santabarbaraca.com

Brooklyn Tourism www.visitbrooklyn.org/

Texas Tourism http://texastourism.com/

Las Vegas http://www.visitlasvegas.com.au/

Tourism Oregon http://traveloregon.com/

Washington DC Mall Area http://washington.org/DC-guide-to/
national-mall

Santa Monica California www.santamonica.com/

New York City www.nycgo.com/

Portland, Oregon www.travelportland.com/

Louisiana www.louisianatravel.com

Florida www.visitflorida.com

Arizona Office of Tourism www.arizonaguide.com

Utah www.utah.com/

Tombstone, Cochise County, Arizona www.explorecochise.com

Moab Tourism www.discovermoab.com

Temecula, California www.temeculacvb.com

Badlands National Park www.nps.gov/badl/index.htm

Los Angeles www.discoverlosangeles.com

West Hollywood www.visitwesthollywood.com

Shopping Till Ya Drop

Macys Discount Card http://www.visitmacysusa.com/visitors/savings.cfm

http://www.macys.com/store/about/visitor/index.jsp

Mall of America http://www.mallofamerica.com/

Shop America Alliance http://www.shopamericatours.com/

FAO Schwartz Toys http://www.fao.com/home/

WalMart America http://www.walmart.com/

South Coast Plaza California http://www.southcoastplaza.com/

Rodeo Drive Shops Beverly Hills http://www.rodeodrive-bh.com/

Powell's Books Portland, Oregon http://www.powells.com/

Target Stores www.target.com/

K Mart Stores www.kmart.com/

Bedding Down Beautifully

The Beacon Hotel NYC www.beaconhotel.com

The Wellington Hotel NYC http://wellingtonhotel.com/

The Handlery Hotels San Francisco and San Diego www.handlery.com/

Cavallo Point Lodge Sausalito/SFO www.cavallopoint.com/

Post Ranch Inn Big Sur www.postranchinn.com/

The Tropicana Resort Las Vegas www.troplv.com/

The Cosmopolitan Las Vegas www.cosmopolitanlasvegas.com/

Topock Rt. 66 Spa & Resort www.topock66.com

The Hacienda Hotel LAX www.haciendahotel.com/

Bacarra Resort & Spa Santa Barbara www.bacararesort.com/

Fess Parker Inn Santa Barbara /www.fessparkerinn.com/

Wahweap Lodge & Houseboats Lake Powell Arizona www.
lakepowell.com/accommodations/wahweap-resort-
accommodations.aspx

The Occidental Hotel, Buffalo Wyoming http://occidentalwyoming.com/

The Rusty Parrot Jackson Hole Wyoming http://www.rustyparrot.com/

The Rustic Inn, Jackson Hole Wyoming www.rusticinnatjh.com/

Ritz Carlton Key Biscayne Florida www.ritzcarlton.com

Cypress House Key West Florida www.historickeywestinns.com/the-
inns/cypress-house/

Shangri La Hotel Santa Monica www.shangrila-hotel.com/

Tanque Verde Ranch, Tucson, Arizona http://tanqueverderanch.com/

El Capitan Cabins Resort , California www.elcapitancanyon.com/
accommodations/canyon-cedar-cabins

Camping and RV Resorts

Borrego Springs RV Resort www.springsatborrego.com

Pirate's Cove RV Resort https://piratecoveresort.com/

Zephyr Cove Resort RV Park & Campground www.zephyrcove.com/
accommodations/zephyr-rv-campground.aspx

Monument Valley Trading Post, Lodge & Tours www.gouldings.com

Whistler Gulch RV Park, Deadwood www.whistlergultch.com

Yellowstone Campgrounds www.nps.gov/yell/planyourvisit/
feesandreservations.htm

Top-Tours and Sightseeing

The Urban Safari www.theurbansafari.com

A Slice of Brooklyn Pizza Tours www.asliceofbrooklyn.com

CityPass www.citypass.com

Elite Special Event Tours www.eliteset.com.au

APT Touring www.aptouring.com

Route 66 Tours www.eleteset.com.au

Starline Sightseeing Bus Tours www.starlinetours.com/

TrekAmerica Tours www.trekamerica.com

Cash, Travel Coverage and Credit Cards

HiFX Currency exchange www.hifx.com.au

Covermore Travel Insurance www.covermore.com.au

AMEX https://www.americanexpress.com/

VISA www.visa.com/globalgateway/gg_selectcountry.jsp

Mastercard www.mastercard.com/index.html

Favored Tail-feathers; Flying

United Airlines www.untied.com

Virgin Airlines www.virgin.com/gateways/virginairlines

Air New Zealand www.airnewzealand.com.au/

Qantas www.qantas.com.au/travel/airlines/home/au/en

Delta Airlines www.delta.com/

Hawaiian Airlines www.hawaiianairlines.com.au/

Virgin Atlantic www.virgin-atlantic.com

Air Tahiti Nui www.airtahitinui.com/

American Airlines www.aa.com/international/

Fiji Airlines www.fijiairways.com

Remarkable Parks!

The National Parks Service http://www.nps.gov

Yosemite National Park http://www.yosemitepark.com/

Yellowstone National Park http://www.yellowstonenationalpark.com/

Central Park NYC http://www.centralpark.com/

About Mark Sheehan

Mark William Sheehan and Hayley

Mark William Sheehan has spent most of his professional career promoting travel to his beloved America. He worked as a writer for a number of American newspapers and magazines, spent years on the road writing tour guides for professional tour directors, and has covered close to 3 million miles of America. Mark's expertise in America has spawned a number of American travel operators and outfits from adventure camping holidays to deluxe motor coach tours and specialty travel options for independent travel.

Mark is a certified 'American specialist' living between a home in the USA and Sydney, Australia.

About Shane Boocock

Shane Boocock is a freelance writer, editor and photographer who has been infatuated with America for over 30 years. Hailing from the North of England originally, Shane now resides in New Zealand when not touring the USA. A former veteran tour guide with TrekAmerica he continues to spend months of the year in America's outdoors and cities capturing images of America. Reach out to Shane if you like on www.iTravelWriter.com or email Shane at itravelwriter@gmail.com

About Bridget Willis

Bridget Willis started her photographic collection of America while traveling around the States as a backpacker, and trekker. Working as a travel consultant in Capetown, South Africa, Bridget would work a while, travel to the USA, and stay until film and funds ran out. Bridget has traveled more of America than most Americans, listing the national parks and the American people as the country's most powerful calling cards.

About Holly O'Sullivan

Holly started travelling with her parents when she was four months old, and now at 18 years, the travel bug is well and truly entrenched. During her gap year, Holly set off for her dream destination: North America. Travelling on her own for the very first time, she carried her back-pack across the U.S. snapping landscapes, cityscapes and engaging the 'locals' along the way. Holly captured anything with her cameras that caught her eye. Keep up with her travels on her blog: http://holly-the-traveller.tumblr.com/

A Whopping Big Thank You!

This book was not created in a vacuum, but to say thank you to everyone who'd had a hand in it might take some time in the telling. I'd like to acknowledge a number of organizations such as Travmedia, California Tourism, Visit Nevada, the great folks at Tourism North Dakota, Colorado, and Wyoming, Visit New York & Company!, Tourism Hawaii, Mike Free, Montana, Idaho, Visit Florida, the Visit USA committee, and the Tourism Industry Association of America.

The book was made better by having some fine photos to go alongside the copy and I'm most grateful to Shane Boocock and Bridget Willis for chipping in some great images. Also offering up happy snaps and valuable feedback were Gordon Swire, Michael and Yon Shin Willis, Anne and Jim Olsen, Remi and Laura Bouskila, Meghan Sheehan, and Cathy Leslie, and my three offspring, Dylan, Hayley, and Cody.

And last but in no way least, are my publishing pals: thanks to the entire team at New Holland Publishers. They have been wonderful, no, make that brilliant!

Published in 2014 by
New Holland Publishers (Australia) Pty Ltd
Sydney • Auckland • London • Cape Town

First published in 2009.

www.newhollandpublishers.com

The Chandlery Unit 114 50 Westminster Bridge Road London SE1 7QY United Kingdom
1/66 Gibbes Street Chatswood NSW 2067 Australia
Wembley Square First Floor Solan Road Gardens Cape Town 8001 South Africa
218 Lake Road Northcote Auckland New Zealand

A record of this book is held at the National Library of Australia.

ISBN: 9781742575193

Managing director: Fiona Schultz
Project editor: Christine Chua
Designer: Hayley Norman
Production director: Olga Dementiev
Printer: Toppan Leefung Printing Ltd (China)

Keep up with New Holland Publishers on Facebook
www.facebook.com/NewHollandPublishers